POETRY
now

Picture A Place

Edited by

Rebecca Mee

First published in Great Britain in 2001 by
POETRY NOW
Remus House,
Coltsfoot Drive,
Peterborough, PE2 9JX
Telephone (01733) 898101
Fax (01733) 313524

HB ISBN 0 75432 674 8
SB ISBN 0 75432 675 6

FOREWORD

Although we are a nation of poets we are accused of not reading poetry, or buying poetry books. After many years of listening to the incessant gripes of poetry publishers, I can only assume that the books they publish, in general, are books that most people do not want to read.

Poetry should not be obscure, introverted, and as cryptic as a crossword puzzle: it is the poet's duty to reach out and embrace the world.

The world owes the poet nothing and we should not be expected to dig and delve into a rambling discourse searching for some inner meaning.

The reason we write poetry (and almost all of us do) is because we want to communicate: an ideal; an idea; or a specific feeling. Poetry is as essential in communication, as a letter; a radio; a telephone, and the main criterion for selecting the poems in this anthology is very simple: they communicate.

CONTENTS

GRANITE COUNTRY

Gorse and heather colour granite country,
where inherent sculpture of huge boulders
thrown by giants are a natural part of landscape.

Abandoned engine houses
silhouette the skyline like thumbs up signals
for all who worked above and below grass.

Men Scryfa, an inscribed stone pillar,
the height of Royal Raven marks the spot this prince
fought and died trying to regain his father's territory.

The earth covering chambered tombs has gone,
now wind echoes through these massive quoits
whispering past secrets of kings and warriors.

The circle stone of Men an Tol
has been threaded with the hopes
of young and old believing in its healing power.

History sleeps in forts and fogous,
folklore of maidens daring to dance
on the Sabbath lives in stone circles.

Life and legend side by side
in granite country is a waking reality
in this place of dreams for a proud Celtic people.

Les Merton

ANAMORPHOSIS

(For Jo)

Come, ride again among Spanish flowers
and dance upon those mountain slopes in spring,
let peace pervade our souls with tranquil hours,
revitalise our lives with freedom's ring;
holding hands we'll stroll in gentle breeze,
scent fragrant sage and thyme upon the air,
cast obligation's bloody chains that squeeze,
lest twilight catch us slowing and ensnare:
time's challis frays with hem unravelling,
its gossamer a phosphorescent trail
of voices within, for they are cavelling,
close tight your eyes, let the dream prevail:
    see crags of blissful soaring birds of prey,
    hold tight my dream, we too are far away.

Bridie Bonello

A Place Called Tomorrow

Flames flicker on faces, still;
bonfire burns upon the hill.
I close my eyes
to take me there.
I feel the burn
but do not care.

She walks with me, in somewhere new;
where life is sweet, and I am too.
The roads run straight
and I feel OK.
When the smoke clears
I'll walk that way.

And the fire fades, from light so bright;
my mind drifts on, to a distant height.
And my girl is there
on a silver beach.
For fleeting moments
she's within reach.

But all things end, ain't that true?
Even dreams, the fire burns through.
So please hold my hand
to quell the doubt.
For the ride is short:
you must breathe out.

Henry Knight

Dreaming Of Control

My mind is often a shelter
from the wrath of reality
Secret fears bring silent tears
when I lose control of myself.
I revert to a land
where nothing I do fails
I leave heroic trails in fairy tales
I'm a vision of accomplishment
Hear me pitch my tent
Here I am content.
I take control of the main event
The life I own is fully grown
but diverts to the time of a child
This is where I hide
Impossible to find
when times are unkind.

John Beals

THOMAS

I chose a place to be with the sea
In silent meditation.
A place of rock, hard gained,
Secret from all ears and eyes
Save only the pulsing knock of the sea.
Withdrew in silent contemplation.
And heard within another's voice,
'Only can you catch through me
the ocean's song and mystery.'

With awe at my random yet unerring choice
I felt the presence in the rocks rise up
Like a mighty mythic being,
Egyptian bird, Pharoah, Indian Queen
Brooding over carapace of sea bird,
Over dead husks of sea life washed
Into the dulled edge of foam.
And rising from the stones
An ancient faery place, a temple,
Where within twelve silent watchers sat.

Dreaming, drifting. Now sudden doubting,
Sensing tang of stinging salt upon the tongue,
O! man, this cannot be.
And then another voice:
'O man indeed! For even now
If the Son of God
In all His glory were to come
Into this place,
You would not see.'

Margaret Gill

DREAM-CATCHER

Upon the windblown moor
Above the lochan,
Where the black grouse held his lek,
Her daughter found the feathers;
Black and curled, momentoes
Of the early morning's passion.

And she wove a dream-catcher.

Teardrops
In a spider's web
Within a silver circle.
From its base she hung the feathers,
Where they caught the evening breeze
And spun the circle
Back and forth.
The dreams were carried on the air
And, trapped within the circle,
Paused
And fell upon the sleeping form below.

And now she walked,
The mother,
Through the evening's softness,
'Mid the sharp perfumes of spring,
The trees and chimneys black against the sky
Which trapped the last of light
And start of night.

The night reminded,
And the mother knew,
That dreams still lingered in the gentle wind,
Awaiting trapment in the web
Among the teardrops.

Dee Yates

THE GOLDEN SEAL

The westerly wind
Lashed wet strands of hair
Against my face,
As I sat cocooned
Waiting for your return.

From a distance
Where the sea enters the loch
A golded streak divides the water,
Followed with my eyes
The ripples getting close.

I could have touched
The sleek curves
Of your golden form,
Caressed your whiskers
With my face -
Dare I interpose upon your solitude?

The wind returned the peace,
Brought out the sun,
And you -
Revelled in the brief moment
Of heat
Glistening against the rock.

A rare sighting you are to me
Who has sat upon this craggy mound
Each year waiting for your return.
The sound you hear is carried in the breeze
A lullaby to the golden seal,
Who remembered me,
And cried.

Suzette Virginia Floyed

VICTORIAN SCENE

The hansom slid, slipped, slithered away, wheels
Crushing the soft snow, soundlessly; she stood,
Shivering, not entirely due to cold.

She knew, he had left something of himself
Behind, sure of that, but too soon to feel
The flutter-kick. That would come later on.

Certain, she knew, he left behind a jewel,
A thing precious from him, but burden too
For her. The loss of job, of family,
She would not consider; she had been his
For eternity in a few moments.
Now her loneliness; now she watched as that,
That cold cab crushing the uncomplaining
Snow, slow-moving over the icy ground
Took him with it, and inside him the piece
Of her that never would return.

Paul A Reeves

POINTING THE WAY

The Hansom cab drew slowly away
Wheels furrowing fallen snow
As if pointing the way of his journey
Such a long way to go.
To join his regiment then board a ship
To sail away into the night
To a land halfway across the world
For Queen and country he would fight.
To the dangerous northern frontiers of India
He would serve with his men
She shivered as she suddenly thought
'Will I ever see you again?'
Sobbing she turned, as the cab disappeared,
To her father who hugged her tight
'Have no fear for he is a very brave man
Everything will turn out right.'
And by candlelight she sat, pen in hand
By her bedside, his portrait near
She composed her letter, the first of many
'My Edward, dearest dear.'
For two long years she wrote, and he to her
At last came her longed for reply
'Oh Father, Father, he's on his way home.'
The tears welled up in her eyes.
On a cold December morn he leaped from a cab
They embraced, to part no more
The cab's tracks in the snow at his journey's end,
Had stopped right outside her door.

Mike Jackson

ON SILENT SNOW

I call your name through the blanketed night,
'Cross the snow carpeted city, stark and white,
My cold feet crunching in icy plight
As the carriage draws you away.

Heartless buildings and leafless trees
Stand still, silent in the whispering breeze,
Hurrying petticoats stiffen and freeze
As the carriage draws you away.

The wide street swallows my wallowing tears,
Horse hooves muted by its slushy veneer,
Night wanderers pass in ignorant fear
As the carriage draws you away.

Wheel tracks, freshly frosted, glisten
In the silvery moonlit mist, and
I call but you no longer listen
As the carriage draws you away.

Frances Pallett

I Was There

Opulence emerged apparent amid
    the snowbound streets of Burgundy.
Gentlemen and ladies strolled to and fro
    like royalty.
Oh for such elegance, such grandeur
    to be mine.
I closed my eyes and I was there.

Roadside trees proudly kiss the ashen sky,
    as if in respect for such an abundance
        of prosperity.
Walkers tiptoed along as if in fear of
    downtreading such underfoot splendour.
Oh for just an hour to savour such
    magnificence.
I closed my eyes and I was there.

A town which discarded all care
    liken to a Christmas card - so embracing.
The essence of dreams.
The joys of fulfilment.
Victorian euphoria in all its glory shines.
I feel so at peace now
    because I know I was there.

Steve Kettlewell

BE INSPIRED

As I glance at the scene many things can I find,
Stories of long ago come rushing to mind.
A carriage on the roadway -
So stately and so gay.
Snow clad streets and mists,
A life so full of bliss
Trees planted along the street -
And people lingered for the life was so sweet.
A leisurely pace when one could stop and think,
And words of kindness forged a link.

Betty Green

MAGIC CARPET

Many a carriage trots down the street
As winter grips the town
Ladies careful where they put their feet
Clouds seem to wear a frown

Gentleman in a greatcoat and top hat
Collar high against the cold
While another not so well attired as that
Steps forth nonchalantly bold

Among the stark bare poplar trees
Daytime errands being done
Buildings decorated with a snowy frieze
Children sledding having fun

With bright white snow muffling sound
Painting a pristine scene
Casts a magic carpet on the ground
Makes dirty streets look clean.

Jennifer A Major

TRANQUILLITY

Feel the stillness,
and the quiet.
Footsteps make no sound
as they pursue the
snowy ground.
Carriage wheels turn
taking Lord and Lady
on their way.
Where they are going
they do not say.
The snow lays thick
upon the trees
and on the paths.
The birds' tiny feet
make impressions in
the snow
and in the park
children hurry home
before it's dark.

Barbara Appèl

Who Will Buy

(Christmas 1886)

From the mullion window - I watch
the world and his wife go by
the busy lanes - bustle with life.
Chestnut sellers - the brazier - glows red
hansom cabs, children in rags, nannies with prams
flower girls, baker's boy, pickpockets, costermonger's lamps,
everyone trying to make an honest bob
the trundles hung high, dressed in holly and ivy
a sprig of mistletoe hangs over the pantry door
cards by penny post - presents are made
the cleaned black lead grate - shines in the lamp's glow
frozen footsteps lie deep where carollers trod.
Once this harsh winter has passed
come June it'll be the Queen's Jubilee
the deep snowy lanes fall silent
soon the Bells of Bow foretell of Christmas
now it's food to prepare, table to lay, goose to roast
from the mullion window - snow's falling again - silently.

David Charles

The Fall

Silently snow has fallen
and dawn reveals a landscape
clothed in a warm white coat.

Beautiful those trees
whose branches with seeming fragility
defy the wintry sky.

Very brave one rose,
leafless and solitary,
petals jewelled with frost.

Plump rounded pillows
formed on the eaves
inevitably soon will fall.

A circling investigating bird
does not descend, but swiftly returns
to the safe place it had left.

Quiet, my heart.

Louise Rogers

Times Past

In days gone by
Under leaden sky
The snow lies thickly upon the ground.
Lady in long gown
Walks through the town
Her footsteps never make a sound.

Horse and cart,
Play their part
In this scene from long ago.
They slip and slide
From side to side
As they trundle through the snow.

No bright lights
Or festive sights
That Christmas time would bring
Hardship lays
In cold dark days
Until the blossoming of spring.

Lynne Walden

A Woman Abandoned

(A Victorian Melodrama)

Alone she stood, in solitude,
A forlorn female in the street
He'd tried his best not to be rude,
But her sad heart had skipped a beat

He had gently let her down
- Said . . . 'He had a wife at home,'
She was just his 'bit in town',
- 'Always had a yen to roam'.
She thought he was a single man
Who'd promised love and marriage.
But he'd lied, then off he'd ran,
Back to his waiting carriage.

She watched the wheels turn in the snow,
As out of sight he sped.
Then proudly turned around to go
Remembering all he'd said.

The tears came slowly down her face,
Her future was no more.
She walked on at a faster pace,
And from her hand she tore,
The ring which he had given her
To seal their loving bond.
She threw it full of anger,
Into the river beyond.

She climbed the snow-capped railings,
With a loud and plaintive cry
She leapt from the bridge, strength failing,
Into dark depths to die.

So ladies, always *do* be sure
Before you love your paramour.

Carol-Anne Marsh

Snowy Days

It's been a very busy day
My toes, my fingers and my nose are oh so very cold.
My thoughts are winging homewards
To family, food and fire.

I see that lucky person
Driving slowly on their way,
Wrapped up in furs and blankets
To drive the cold away.

And yet I know I'm lucky
With a warm coat on my back.
That poor man crossing over
Must feel the cold so bad.

The snow looks oh so pretty
As it gently falls to earth
But oh the problems when we come
Our homeward way to wend.

Nessie Shaw

Snow Scene

Wading through white,
Falling through snow,
Losing the pathway,
Nowhere to go.

Standing and covered,
Trapped but content,
Watching the heaven,
From which it was sent.

Lee Severns

Memories Of Time

Dim the gas lamps at eventide
Footprints of high heeled buttoned boots
Smudged by a long black dress dragging in the snow
Took me back to my dreams of gentlemen in suits
Closing my eyes I once again saw a brush bursting through a chimney
Soot falling, sprinkling black specks upon snow
I hear the squeal of children's voices as they clap hands
Making a wish only they must know
Around the corner silently came a handsome carriage
Wheels muffled by the snow's depth
Leaving a curved trail, driven by a top hatted driver
Floating away in another time I hold my breath
Can I help you cross the road my lady
Beside me was a tall man bowing, hat in hand
He took my arm as I held my long dress above the snow
Smiling I thank him feeling so enriched and grand
My heart fluttered, I was in the nineteenth century
Around me everything seemed quiet
Trees were still, no leaves, who was I
Perhaps I was a suffragette in a time warp, why
No this could not be, I would not be helped across the road
A gentleman would not wish to know me
With a gasp I slowly opened both eyes
Looking out of the window there was the snow
Fading away I saw a lady in the same black dress
Smiling up at me was my grandmother
Words reached me, I wanted to see you my child
For a few seconds I had been her, as one we were together
One black boot button lay upon the snow
I would remember this forever.

Elizabeth Cowley-Guscott

THE PHOTO

In one hundred years from now,
People will view this photo,
And think it's very nice.

'Look at the clothes',
They'll all say and,
'Look at the car',
They'll encourage.

They'll just see the scene.
No people. No lives.
We'll just be part of the scene.
They won't believe we lived,
Breathed, sang, laughed and cried.

The snow will make it picture perfect,
But it just makes our fingers freeze.
The buildings will be historic architecture,
Not out houses. Not our homes.

In one hundred years from now,
It'll be just an old picture,
Not a once living scene.

Kimberly Jamie

CASTING THOUGHTS OF VICTORIAN DAYS

Winter days of long ago
When you walked most of the time,
In the deepest of snow
The gentlemen and ladies so fine
Dressed up in their best, most of the time.

In days gone by, there were the upper class
The middle class and the poor.
You could tell by the way they dressed up
If they were rich or if they were poor.

The rich got around in a coach or trap
The rest would walk everywhere
But these were the ways of Victorian days
Class distinction, it was always there.

The snow scenes of long ago
Were perfect, and a delight
Because you hadn't got a snow plough
To break up the peaceful sight.

The scene in this small picture
Its where rich folk, I think would stay
Going about their morning business
On a bright cold winter's day.

I always liked their winter clothes
Fur hats and sometimes muffs
They always seemed to have plenty of time
And never in a rush.

Looking at the horse and trap
And the folks around the street
Could be doing early morning shopping
Before there's more people on the street.

Florrie Macgruer

ENIGMA (OF A PICTURE)

He turns away and she lifts her skirt as she goes,
Stepping daintily through the snow with no fuss.
Even when passions run high, still a lady knows
How to comport herself as a lady does.

What words may have passed between them here on the street?
(We can but guess some scarlet sin or disgrace).
What whispers of love or anger? Or did they meet
To plan some reckless tryst in a secret place?

The world goes on around them; the coach rattles by.
People pass on to the business of their day.
Skeletal trees stretch tall to the greying sky.
Woman and man go each on their separate way.

Jackie Lapidge

Passing Strangers!

Winter's snow upon the ground
Bringing chaos everywhere,
Hansom cabs hurrying by
No time to spare.

In long black coat and tall top hat
A gentleman heads home
Hurrying from a clandestine assignation, perhaps?
With the lady of means, cosily clad,
Have they just alighted from the Hansom cab?

Head down, she treads her way carefully through the snow
Reluctant perhaps to leave her beau
But, alas it seems, for him, the tryst was one of many
He turns away from poor Jenny.

The cab ploughs its way through the snow
Has the coachman a long way to go?
Heading his cab down the tree lined street,
Looking for customers, he's yet to meet.

Out of the corner of his eye, he spots a workman,
Is he a fare? The cabbie's not certain,
A well bustled lady waits on his right
If he could make this his last fare
He could call it a night.

Joan Creary

HOMEWARD BOUND

The snow fell in the night.
As silent as a ghost it drifted into hollows and softened
all the contours while the town's folk were asleep.
People emerged from their homes in the morning
to find it lying pristine and deep.
The sun glinting on roofs and treetops had transformed
the town into a jewelled grotto, beneath a sky of cerulean blue.
And the new world shimmered in the brilliant light.

Now in late afternoon that same sky had a menacing aspect,
The passing cabs, with their wheels and horses hooves silenced
by the muffling snow were gliding by like spectres.
Who were they carrying behind their darkened windows?
Whose eyes were watching the homeward bound travellers
struggling through the treacherous snow and what were
their conjectures?
Did that young man in workman's attire, have the intention of
snatching her bag as he stepped off the pavement in front of her
causing her to start.
And was the sound of following footsteps real or the frantic
beating of her heart?

In the gloom of the coming evening, dark pockets of deep shadow
formed between the buildings, and to her over-stretched imagination
these harboured all sorts of undesirables.
She tried to quicken her pace but was hampered by the wet hem
of her trailing gown.
Never had she wanted so desperately to get away from the town
Her small garret room from which she had escaped so joyfully
just hours ago, now seemed like the most desirable place to be.

Gwendoline Bennett

AND YET

I think I see you standing there
  and yet
    and yet

I know that cannot be
Our last goodbye
Was said three times

But still I long
  and hope
    and pray

You will come back to me.

Only my yearning
Fills the place
Where you once stood.

So how long
Must I wait
Before my heart accepts

You will not come back to me
  and yet
    and yet

Perhaps . . .

Mary Petrie

THAT FATEFUL DAY

Our lives will never turn out, quite as we expect.
We see that fate can intervene when in retrospect.
Twists of life could lead to pain, to sorrow or relief.
While fateful turns may even lead to heartache or to grief.
The auspicious day that is forever etched upon my mind,
Was when Godfrey was my love, and I was so blind.

The sky was grey and heavy, the landscape dark and bleak.
It was a portent of the havoc that he soon would wreak.
My toes like ice were frozen then, the snow crunched under boot.
New winds of change had blown on me, I saw he was a brute.
He'd made me many promises, so callously and cool,
And now that he was leaving me, I felt an awful fool.

I tried to run behind the coach, along the lined wheel track,
I was bereft, no time to pack, I tried to bring him back.
There were people all around me, but none of them could see.
They went about their business, they had no time for me.
They weren't aware of my sad face, my panic or my plight.
They paid no heed and scurried on, in the wintry light.

When the coach had gathered speed, I stood there in the street,
I stood frozen on the spot, frozen head to feet.
It took many years before my pain had almost gone,
Then I found somebody else, a man who really shone.
Then one day I saw that Godfrey's picture had appeared,
It was on the front page of the paper, it was weird!

He had been condemned to death, it was his final day,
I was shocked, quite overcome, there were no words to say.
He had married several times and murdered every wife,
The wives were old and wealthy, but he envied them, their life.
I saw that fate had looked on me, I had no claim to wealth.
It seemed that luck was on my side, I still had my health.

Vivienne E Cirelle

COLD COMFORT

How quickly my day of rest has passed
Dark sky leaden and overcast.
The hem of my dress drags in the snow
My cold, cold feet know where to go.

The master seated beside the fire
Harkening to a heavenly choir
Christmastide with holly and berry
Beneath the fir tree gracious and merry.

But for me just a bare damp room
Where I'll spend my time after festive noon
I will gaze from my window and hear robin sing
On this winter day, head tucked 'neath his wing.

My dear little sister will miss me dearly
I have sent her wishes so sincerely.
I vow one day in a coach I'll arrive
To be welcomed by family at Christmastide.

Gifts and boxes in scarlet red
And a beautiful bonnet upon my head
A dress of silk and a shining ring
Choirs of angels for me will sing.

But now I rest on my coverlet white
A candle to light me to bed each night
I dream of the day when my boat comes in
And all the world is free from sin.

Jennifer H Fox

MEMORIES IN A PICTURE

Memories of my childhood
Oh! So long ago.
When we had four seasons
And in the winter snow.
Oh, those happy days of yore!

They stay forever young.

When I was small
And life was new

And time had just begun.

Gladys Mary Gayler

A PICTURE RECALLS TIME

The picture dissolves, reforms and briefly regresses,
its subjects, men and women, emerging from kitchens and living
rooms where coal fires glowed in grates and open fire places.
Bowls of steaming porridge had warmed them.
Somewhere now, a phonograph plays, its tones and voices
dissonant to the ears of the 3rd Millennium.
Snow-muffled, the thud of hooves from the hackney's horse
are engulfed soon in the mélee of a busier thoroughfare:
top hats teem in the bobbing tide and reflect the wintry sun;
bustled women, some veiled, pick their way slowly,
walking canes, silver topped, prodding the snowy pavement.
Somewhere from the spawning mass a Cockney voice extols:
'Buy my loverly violets, ladies - loverly violets!'
Cloth-capped, muffler-wrapped, a newsboy's hoarse cry
proclaims events in South Africa.
From a side street come the gleeful shouts of urchins in colourfully
adorned, patched trousers, as they pelt each other with snowballs;
a yapping mongrel leaps to tug at dangling scarves.
Around the corner, hand-bell tolling, a hand-cart emerges,
as housewives respond occasionally with bundles of woollens,
gratefully accepting the coins pressed into their palms.
On the busy thoroughfare again, a hackney carriage bears its fare,
'To Baker Street, my deah fellow!'
Truncheon dangling, in high-collared coat, a policeman calls
to a maid, rug shaking, at an upstairs window,
his wink larger than his handle bar moustache!
Street women, clientele discreetly behind, walk smiling to 'Madam's'.
Now the scene hazes in the yellowing smog of innumerable chimneys,
as the lamp lighter, with long pole, switches on the gas lamps.

Ron Hails

A Christmas Tale

Christmas Day tomorrow, and I don't know what to do;
  Got the sack and daren't tell the wife.
Haven't bought a turkey and I couldn't get a goose;
  It's the worst of Christmas Eves in all my life.

I see them in their hansoms with their good boots and their furs.
  They never give a thought to folks like me.
My wife thinks I'm a wonder. She deserves a better life -
  The way we live, it breaks my heart to see.

I'll have to tell her somehow, but will she understand
  how I'd rather risk the sack than bow and scrape?
'Sweet Jesus, on your birthday will you spare a thought for us -
  Must we always live like this, with no escape?'

Why, what's this? I see her running, and she's calling out my name.
  She's holding up a paper in her hand.
She's looking so excited. 'It's my cousin Jack,' she cries,
  'he's found a place for you - oh, ain't that grand?'

'Oh, Bill, let's go tonight,' she says, 'and stay with cousin Jack.
  We can have our Christmas there with him and May.'
'Thank you, Lord,' I think, 'for listening', and I give my Beth a hug.
  Our new life begins tomorrow - Christmas Day.

Patricia Fallace

Was Led

Enhancing each heartbeat,
And letting preach,
To soul;
A dawning.

The painter,
Shirtless,
Dressed in spiritual, calm;
Captured the essence,
In nature's, sweet touch.

Each stroke, of brush,
Echoed;
The fertility,
Full froth,
Sheer wonder.

Was led,
By song in vein;
To the beauty,
In world, generously alive.

Rowland Warambwa

A PRETTY PICTURE

New York or Olde Englande, in the stage setting
for an Oscar Wilde film.
'Make sure that you tread carefully in that snow,
as you rush past in the bustling little town to buy possessions!'
'Mind how you lift that skirt and reveal those pretty
white ankles in those pick-wicker boots!'
Such gallantry I'm sure for a young paper boy,
'Now out after a night of cahoots!'

Colette Breeze

CHEERY LITTLE TOWN

Cheery little town,
Sweet little town.
Pretty little people,
Walking up and down.
Bustling busy bodies
Bagging better bargains.
Beautiful, bonny babies
Bouncing in their buggies.
Laughing little grandmas
Holding children's hands.
Dippy, doting daddies
Wrestling with their shopping.
Bossy, battling mummies
Trying to keep order.
Snappy dressed up grandads
Looking out of place,
Sneaking out of family circles
Looking for an empty space
To unwind. Let's be kind
And let them find their place.
A town of topsy-turvy characters
Walking up and down.
Sweet little town
Cheery little town.

Joan E Blissett

Comparisons

A horse-drawn carriage rumbles through the snow,
Ladies in long dresses tread carefully as they go.
Holding up their skirts to keep them dry and neat,
Laced ankle boots upon their dainty feet.

Further up the road, a man with besom broom,
Strives to clear a pathway to his door.
A man with hands in pockets surveys the wintry scene,
Hoping it will end soon, when comes the thaw.

What a difference in our world of today.
When snow appears, the snow ploughs clear the way.
Ladies wear high boots and trousers to keep warm.
Life is better in 2001, when there is a snow storm.

Alma Scorer

A WINTER'S TALE

The muffled wheels rumbled in the snow,
The ladies skirts swished,
The boys' footsteps crunched
No hoops could bowl,
No fivestones played in the gutter.

The Hansom cab continued its journey,
The ladies skirts got wet,
The boys' heads down, now trudged along,
A warm mug to revive, some,
A shivering cold night, to endure, for the gutter gang.

Gill Mainwaring

Stillness Of Time

Are the clouds full of rain or snow?
All those people with places to go
Wrapped up warm against the cold
Can't pick out who's young or old
The trees are bare, like large twigs to the sky
What secrets lurk beneath the snow and lies
Wheels making tracks upon the ground
Footsteps prints turning up all around
A man takes a step from path to the street
Hands in pocket feels incomplete
Has he a job to go to during the day,
Or is boredom setting in and he's wasting away?
The man on the right is walking fast
Warm fire awaiting at home at last
The lady is dressed from top to toe
No money worries, no tales of woe
I wonder what's going on behind closed doors
My imagination inspired from water and oils.
The artist has captured the stillness of the time
I wish I owned it, I wish it was mine.

Jan Nice

WALK

Ambling down history's memory lane,
As the clicking steps of folk in snowy street,
Trundle turning carriage wheel, clip-clop hoof.
Varied tales of another age ignite.

Snow, cosy furs created their beauty,
Just as good as in summer season.
Horses' breath elegantly spiralling in frosty air,
As crack curled whip stating their trot.

White linened tables, polished mahogany,
Soft candle light glinting silver and glass,
Elegantly sipping the fizz, anticipation
'Ladies and gentlemen, dinner is served!'

Song, dance, ballgowns glitter,
White gloves, dainty heels, dressed hair,
Tailed gowned gentlemen, hand proffered,
'Allow me Madam, may we dance?'

Log fires warming glow, mystical light,
Embuing panels, leather, ornaments bright,
Cosy filled hearts, smiling with pleasure,
Hardly hearing clocks hourly call.

Church bells merrily ringing
Skipping children, smiling folk
Shining sun in bright blue sky above
God's all embracing benevolence eternal.

Anne Mary McMullan

UNTITLED

What a pretty winter's scene of days so long ago,
darkened sky above the trees promising more snow.
Yet - would it have been as picturesque in reality,
or is it only idyllic through our sentimentality?

It looks very pretty, but the truth would have to be,
it brought in its wake for many a tale of misery.
For the very depth of the snow would mean bitter cold temperatures,
with no central heating, it meant calamity.

Pretty frosted patterns upon the windowpanes,
but when the frost is on the inside - cold comfort can be gained!
Coughs and colds and chilblains, bronchitis and pneumonia,
all creep upon those who have no warmth.

With little or no anaesthetics, broken bones such pain would bring
no wonder so many fainted, before even an arm could be put in a sling!
So many illnesses now mostly are gone that were rife about that time,
like smallpox, diphtheria, scarlet fever, too many to mention all in
this rhyme!

Hansom cabs and horses seem romantic as can be,
but families lived closer then - for the main part -
so distance and time were not so much the object possibly!
Could all that seems important now be delivered by a horse and cart?

Infant mortality was horrendous -
even for the nobility.
Large families were had, not for fashion,
but to try to establish the next generation you see.

Wash day must have been a nightmare,
as fingers in the water froze.
No spin dryers, or tumble dryers,
the wind, a candle flame, or fire bare to dry the clothes.

What a pretty winter's scene of days so long ago,
but I'm really not so sure I'd want to swap you know!

Margi Hughes

MELTING MOMENTS

Picking her way carefully,
She and her brother,
Make their way down the avenue,
Through the snow,
To Christelly, number fifty six, steady as you go,

Local children building a snowman,
Throw some snowballs in fun,
Everybody laughed as we hurried inside,
Large oak door closed tight,
Leaving picturesque avenue to its delight,

After removing our coats and hats etc,
We enter the study to find the five family children,
Watching the snow through the window,
Laughing at the antics of the kids outside,
And longing for the chance to slip and slide,

But more pressing matters were at hand,
The pleasures of English literature and their recent essays,
To say nothing of the history of India and China,
Or the Tropics of Cancer and Capricorn,
Were lost, only to the snow outside were they drawn,

So we promised to take the children out into the snow,
Once they'd completed their studies for the day,
With their fathers' permission of course,
This had the desired effect,
A new impetus into their studies the children did inject,

All the children worked very hard,
By three o'clock books were stacked and pencils cased,
Children impatiently fought with wellingtons, gloves and scarves,
At last we were ready, out to the great white wilderness to play,
But bitter disappointment stamped their faces,
When they realised the snow had all but melted away.

P J Littlefield

TIME BEING MINE AND THINE

The air was crisp and cold,
Evening was rapidly descending,
Temperatures were reaching a low ebb,
As preparations were being made
For night-time activities.

Leaving furrows in the snow,
Horse-drawn carriages, passed by,
With only a muffled sound,
As the horses' hooves penetrated the snow,
Carrying the occupants to their destination

The grace and beauty of the crinoline dress,
Was a delight to see,
As skirts were demurely raised,
Avoiding as much snow, possible.

Street markets were closed,
Street vendors were wending their way home,
No doubt planning their next purchase with traders
Early the next morning.

A lone dog gazed enquiringly,
At the huddled human form,
Clutching the strength of hope,
Whose only aspect of survival was a begging cap.

The wealth of the human race
Appears in varying degrees,
Each to discover its occupational pace.
Time, shares a thought
For the homeless needs.

Lorna Tippett

A Road In Snow

A road in snow
So long ago,
A carriage passing
Its thin wheels
It seems
As good as new.

Without vulcanised rubber
No engine throbs.
Did the horse feel cold?
As a child I asked
On seeing the picture.

The elegant lady - in the foreground?
Is the gentleman with her?
Who appears behind a little
Or the coarser man
Who is coming towards her?

Maybe they know each other
And he wishes to invite her
To sit in front of a fire
In a snow covered building,

To warm - to dry her feet
Can't she afford a carriage
Or was she just out for a stroll?
And knows nobody at all.

C J Bayless

Along The Way

See, amid the winter's snow
The people said to me
Will you not tell us
What things are to us?
Then I answered them
The excellency of your strength
The desire of your daughters
Are trooping to the churchyard
They cover their lips
Their ties are upon their necks
And shoes upon their feet
The isles are glittering with lights
Splashing on the fine linen
With broidered work of the women
Lovely song fills the air
A pleasant voice playing well
On an instrument in every building
Tells this is a special day.

Ebenezer Essuman

Winter Weather

The journey was long and treacherous in places
And weariness showed in all of our faces
We arrived at last, near the village green
The snow was so deep the grass couldn't be seen.

We'd come for Christmas to be with our relations
Looking forward to all the celebrations
We picked up our bags and walked in the snow
The easterly wind made our faces glow
We walked in the tracks where horse and cart had been
It was so cold and a very wintry scene.

Ladies in their crinolines were gingerly walking about
Suddenly in the distance there was a shout
One of the ladies had taken a tumble
We rushed to her aid, I'm alright' she managed to mumble.

Gingerly she got up and we brushed her down
There was snow all over her lovely gown
Someone rushed out with a hot drink
She was so grateful and she gave me a wink

We picked up our bags and went on our way
To Granda's and Grandma's where we will stay.

Patricia Youngs

When Summer Fades

When summer days are gone - once more,
When evening darkness appears - evermore
Then I'll take a walk down childhood lane
There to browse and laugh again,
Ah my old chums will really be old by now,
Wonder what they are like, what they do?
As I wander down that long, winding lane
I'm only dreaming until summer comes again,
But as I wander at least I laugh and smile,
For childhood days were the golden ones of life.
My thoughts journey on to many happy holidays,
Mostly taken by the sea, memories that flood back to me,
As I dine and partake another glass of choice wine
I'll ponder slowly along that very long lane;
From my childhood days - to holidays by the sea
Then again to explore many photographs, old and new,
With family and friends - winter can be cosy
You see, for it won't seem very long like this
Before spring will guide back summer again.

Des Lamb

NOT DECEMBER!

For December I do not care
With its dismal chill in the air
Semi-darkness
Leaden skies
Running noses
Watering eyes
Pinched faces peering through the gloom
Longing for home, and a warm room.
Fog and frost liaisons
Salmon-pink horizons
Salt wagons
Spilling out their gritty loads
On dark ice-encrusted roads
And to end
I do not care at all
For that pagan Christmas festival.

Joyce Alice Turner

Too Late

He watched her go
When the immaculate snow
made all the town
Look beautiful and bleak.
What could he say
As she was driven down
To the station? Too late to speak.

Time had been all about
But now time had run out.
Mr Moggs in his top hat
Had been a messenger of doom.
She'd come back engaged.
He hadn't spoken and that
Had been fatal. Here came Miss Groom.

Gillian Bence-Jones

The Poor And The Rich

The shabbily dressed woman crossed the street
Her only dress was trailing in the snow
Getting wet and dirty as the snow was made
Slushy by the wheels of the carriages
Which travelled along the road
She wondered how she would dry the dress
With no money to buy fuel for the fire
Every Friday she would redeem her wedding ring
But by the Monday it was pawned again
To enable her to feed her large family
Her husband toiled long hours for a pittance
But they still lived a meagre existence
She paused to look at the ladies passing by
All were dressed up in their smart clothes
They wouldn't worry if they spoiled them in the snow
They could always buy more and not consider the cost
But then she wondered if any of them were widowed
Or had perhaps lost an only child
She thought of her good husband and six loving children
And realised that she was truly blessed.

Diana Daley

Great-Grandfather's Tale

The old keep many pictures in their hearts,
But one alone is all I ever see:
The same I saw when as a boy of five
I watched that carriage draw away from me.

Dark was the street and dark the very day
They tore apart a mother and her son,
Never to meet again in mortal life.
I do not forgive, but what is done is done.

The aunt who cared for me would not explain
Though I admit she did her best for me.
Slowly, I tried to put the past away
But now I am old, that picture is all I see.

Cold was the day that froze my childish heart,
Even the snow was grey as trodden steel.
I felt the world had turned its back on me:
To this old man that five-year-old is real;

For I am still that child who does not know
Why his own mother was taken from his clasp.
I know that we were weeping, she and I,
But for the rest I have no facts to grasp.

Yet somewhere she waits, and when it is my time,
We shall be reunited and she will explain.
Then, the long sorrow of our parted lives
Will be forgotten with the last of pain.

It will be summer and the coach and pair
Will carry her to me, mile by golden mile,
The winter road shall blossom in full glory
And those who turned their backs will turn and smile.

Pamela Constantine

VICTORIAN WINTER

Footprints carry the echo
Of a land once walked before,
While horses' hooves and carriages
Reveal the road once travelled.

Children play joyfully,
Wrapped in warm clothes and black boots,
Bringing again that certain stillness
Of a day and time, not easily forgotten.

Passers by seem to overshadow
A line of trees with their tallness,
Especially with well-structured walking lines
And with their long coats and tall hats.

The buildings too, echo the day,
With snow-covered rooftops and chimney pots,
While small windows keep out the wind
Of this chilly winter's day.

Huddy

GENERATIONS IN THE SNOW

Evocative dream
To those who see old time
Many year remembrances
Perhaps recall the histories
In picture, music or even rhyme.

The dream past
When wars or peace
Prevailed and time lasted long
In the passing seasons, not knowing
This short lease.

The dream or nightmare
Not seen in this quiet revelation
Of the violence of seasons
Yet to arrive, nor man's treachery
To the future generation.

The dream or rapture
Of happinesses we cannot know
Told in a quiet corner
For us to recall in capture in present
Wish a modern personal drama so.

We tell no tale
There is not tale to tell
From those in daily
Sights or seasons their secrets
Will not sell.

John Amsden

MEMORIES

A winter's tale of long ago,
Of buttoned boots ankle deep in snow
And skirts that skim along the path,
Brushing aside the winter's wrath.
A friendly smile from reddened cheeks,
Small children playing hide-and-seek,
Gas lamps that guide you on your way,
Like guardian angels they light your day.
Puddings wrapped in muslin cloth
And steaming bowls of beef bone broth.
My mother's eyes like embers glow,
Hold memories dear of long ago.

Carroll Abramides

Grandfather's Work

On the box of his cab, it's 1908,
Snow fell on Southampton both early and late.
The two old crossing sweepers swept long and hard,
The snow ne'er abated, so back to the yard.
The cab horse dug in with a fetlock quite thin,
Then touched on a tramline and skidded right in.
Crossed traces, shouting, the poor creature floundered,
'Put a sack on her head,' Grandfather shouted.
Such heaving and pulling the mare to her feet,
This day's work is over, to home they retreat.
A slow walk to Millbrook through deepening snow,
A red gash on her foreleg, dripped very slow.
Hot oats and bran and liniment for rubbing.
It's not the first time this mare's had a drubbing.

Just a glimpse at these days of Edwardian bliss,
But the man in the street his work must not miss.
Cabs for the train folk on Blechynden Terrace,
Brougham for the doctor who sometimes would harass.
Cold days or wet through on the box of his cab,
Sometimes as a treat, pie and port to be had.
The decade rolled by and came 1914,
In the world of the cab great changes were seen.
Motors were coming and horses were fewer,
Except of the coalman, milkman and brewer.
Grandfather retired to a big, spartan house,
The whole family lived there, even a mouse.
Thankfully the old man attained ninety-two,
Enabling grandson to recall it for you.

Denis M Pentlow

The Hush Of Winter

The hush of winter on a snow-laden morn
The quiet of the carriage horse-drawn
As it's carefully steered along the icy street
To take its passengers to their place of meet

The muffled sound of distant talk
As those on foot do carefully walk
Across the road to tree-laden aisles
Where children greet them with cheery smiles
At the thought of sledging in the snow
As they seek a suitable place to go

The shops are full of winter fare
Where some will buy or some will just stare
Longing to enter to feel the warm
Away from the cold into which they were born

The hidden alleys and crowded side streets
That lead from the road where the people meet
Give a different story to the smooth snow-laden way
Where the dampness of slush penetrates a home doorway
Leading to spartan rooms which are barely warm
Where winter brings heartache of another child lost just born

But hope can be found on this winter's day
Through those seeking to help in their charitable way
As the need of those becomes clearer to all
As they take their walk careful not to fall

The hush of winter on a snow-laden morn
The quiet of the carriage horse-drawn
The different people whose paths will meet
As they walk along the icy street

Martine L Shelton

Snow

She waits for the carriage to pass,
Then carefully picks her way over the tracks.
It has snowed again
And the wheels have already churned through the white.
She hurries to meet her mother.
The hem of her skirt is touched by the slush.
Her shoes slide underfoot as she walks on.

Kate Ibbeson

WINTER SCENE

He coughs, stamps feet and chafes his numbed fingers,
Anxious to work on while daylight lingers.
His window frames the scene . . . snow settled down
On roof, on road, on square, muffling the town.
Already sketched out, a wedge of High Street,
Now, dab in shop doorways where gossips meet.
Still on the left, a black carriage, of course,
With unseen passenger, hinted-at horse.
He paints what he sees while half in a trance,
Thick daub here, slash there - take glance after glance.
Slow down. Far right . . . shadowy . . . light less good . . .
Deft suggestion of a prim neighbourhood.
Some blobs, shapes, people walking in the square . ..
Quick, thin wispy strokes for trees growing there . . .
Lastly, he paints her in her long, blue dress
As she goes unknowing past his address.
Dusk. Picture done. Ice-cold pleasure with pain.
Never will he paint such a scene again.

Years since that artist laid aside his brush
To buy his 'Winter Scene' there was no rush,
But times now are changed. He finds it worthwhile,
That inmate of the room now, filled with guile,
To fake both the picture and the artist's name
Before slipping it in a brand new frame.
Not for him suffering through winter - cold,
He finds a dealer and the picture's sold,
After which he strolls across that same square,
Passing picnickers and sunbathers there.

Chris Creedon

CHRISTMAS 1865

It is Christmas Eve 1865,
Christmas shoppers everywhere.
The snow is thick over London town,
Scrooge is on his way home, time to spare.

On his way home to see four ghosts
As mentioned by Charles Dickens.
Christmas past, present and yet to come
And Marley, ghost with chains and chickens

All this happened last century but one,
Christmas was great back then.
No kids demanding costly toys,
All merry, like a big, fat hen.

H G Griffiths

The Day Known As Christmas Eve

We awoke to find a deep blanket of snow; fallen upon us
during the night,
Nature had realised Christmas was near, giving all this great
seasonal sight,
The streets were full of festive cheer, shoppers made their way
thro' snow,
Hansom cabs carried the gentry, but conditions made progress slow.

The markets were very busy; the Christmas spirit was now in
full swing,
Folk stopped for a while on street corners, listening to the
choristers sing,
The children were having a wonderful time, many snowmen they
would build,
Others had home-made sledges; 'twas good to see these youngsters
so thrilled.

The overcast skies gave a stark warning; another snowstorm
was on its way,
And soon that white blanket floated down, but the kiddies
continued to play,
Traders' voices were loud and clear as they relentlessly bawled
their wares,
As the horse-drawn cabs trundled along, safely delivering their fares.

More carol singers take to the streets, 'tis evening, their lanterns aglow,
A crescendo of hooves can be heard, as four-in-hand gallops over
the snow,
Above the strains of 'Noel', the post horn sounds through the cold
night air,
A warning to the folk of York, the stagecoach from London's
almost there.

The coach house greets the passengers, deep snow, but a good
trip nevertheless,
Not a sign of the travellers' scourge, the dreaded Dick Turpin
astride Black Bess,
No time to lose for farrier and groom, the horses must be brushed
and fed,
Then after shoeing and trimming hooves, get new straw for the
stable bed.

The children all bathed and tucked up in bed, the old log fire
burning bright,
Take time to stand in the doorway, look for the star that was a
guiding light,
Reflect on a miracle that made Christmas, how did the
Virgin Mary conceive?
'Tis a busy but wonderful mystical time; the day known as
Christmas Eve.

Wenn-The-Penn

Scene Of Yesteryear

I see snow-clad streets of yesteryear
All crunchy and pure white
With ladies promenading by
A few gentlemen in sight.

Bedecked in clothes of olden times
They take their morning walk
As cabs pass by they meet with friends
And have a little talk.

The tall trees form an avenue
A Winter mantle scene
In Springtime soon this scene will change
'Twill be all pleasant - green.

The ladies in their finery
Elegant and oh so smart
Add a grace and glow for the passing beau
And warm the cockles of your heart.

I love the peace of this quiet time
As the clop of the horses go by
The buildings transformed with their icy roofs
Against the snow-laden sky.

A Winter scene of yesteryear
A Century ago,
Still tugs at your heart and lifts your soul
Encaptured by the snow.

Mollie D Earl

The Picture On The Wall

I saw the picture on the wall,
It fascinated me.
A scene from Russia? So 'twould seem,
No skirts above the knee.
A Horse and coach, a snowbound street,
No cars or high-rise flats to see.
A chilling sight 'neath dull, grey sky,
Long coats, some fur, hung down to feet.
Tall trees in rows, bereft of leaf
In winter's cruel, steel-like grip.
That comes unfailingly each year,
To set the scene, make unwary slip.
Those bygone days of yesteryear,
Depicted by an artist's brush
That spells out details of lives long spent,
Unlike in modern times, no rush.
The picture tells the story
Of what each year doth store,
Of how folk spent their daily lives
In winter, eighteen-eighty-four.

J Blades

Silence

The icy cold had gone, as snow gently fell
Making all clean and white.
The silence was eerie as horses hooves were
Wrapped in sacking so not to slip on icy roads.
People came out of their houses to shop or go to work.
It was not yet Christmas time.
Children were in school, huddled round the
Old black stove to keep warm.
Soon playtime and snowball fights and fun!
But for now, the street was almost empty of sound,
Like a picture postcard of long ago.
Stopped in time.

Jennifer M Trodd

BE INSPIRED

The carriage rattled past her;
It crunched upon the snow.
She was walking out;
She had another path to go

To meet a secret lover.
No one would ever see,
So through the back streets cautiously
She hurried on with glee.

No tracks were down that alley
Which her virgin steps clear marked;
Till she stumbled as she startled
An angry dog which barked.

Footprints were all that could be found;
No trace of where she went
Although the driver recognised
A snap police had sent.

An amateur photographer
Had caught her in his view.
Look closely at this picture
It perhaps could have been you.

Tina Watkin

Winter Regina

Listen.
Can you hear the ice compact beneath the wheels?
Hear the frozen elements resist the pressure?
The crunch of snow beneath the lady's well-placed heels
on treacherous ice; footsteps in careful measure?
Can you hear the whistle, nonchalant, of the young man, hands
in pockets
as he steps out onto the road, no cares abound?
Another picture, painted just a moment later,
would find him wet and humbled on the mocking ground.
Can you hear the still air, oppressive in its silence?
Hear the promise hanging heavy in the skies?
Winter, harsh but necessary, in defiance,
holds sweet treats its cruel exterior belies.
Do you hear the lean trees, in their determination?
They will not buckle 'neath the weight of the snow,
nor snap, when the wind roars in frustration.
They stand calm and tall. They will survive and grow.
Can you hear voices down the street, strangely muted
as if Winter herself demands peace?
Laying down her blanket of white as she lays down her rules
and reigning all, 'til spring demands release.

S P Oldham

Every Picture Tells A Story

A dull November day,
Earth and sky seem to meet
As well-clad, lonesome figures
Carefully plant their snowy feet.
Quite a pleasant area,
A broad pavement-way with trees,
And carriages for the likes of them
That take their life with ease.
There seems to be a casualness
Amongst the figures here,
A chap with hands in pockets
Reflecting time to spare.
The lady has no shopping,
So she's visiting do you think?
The scene is reminiscent
Of skaters on a rink.
The trees, they could be Poplar,
Though bereft of every leaf
They still make a charming avenue
For folk to stroll beneath.
The stillness must be deafening
As you get the snow on snow,
But the picture brings a sense of peace
Enjoyed so long ago.

Gloria Thorne

THE LITTLE RED BUS

Trundling along down the quiet country lane
The little red bus can be seen quite plain
It's the day when folk go shopping to the nearby market town
The village will be empty - nearly all are going down
Loaded with their baskets and coloured shopping bags
Happy wide-eyed children waving tiny flags
What a lot of bother, such a lot of fuss
To seat each one in comfort in the little red bus
The jolly old conductor gave a sharp pull on the bell
It's his way to tell the driver that everything is well
The doors are closed and off they go chugging up the hill
The old bus puffs and pants along and everyone sits still
They've safely made it to the top, the farmer gave a shout
'Gather up your baskets folks, we'll soon be getting out'
Not so very far to go, past the busy water mill
Another bend, a field of corn, then they set off down the hill
The country lanes are left behind, the town looks at its best
At last they reach the station where the little bus will rest
'We'll meet you here at four o'clock,' the old conductor said
'Don't forget your birdseed Joe, and you said you wanted bread'
The farmer's wife dressed in her best is the first one to get down
With just a little walk to reach the centre of the town
Material for a winter's dress and when it's nearly three
She'll meet her friends, and off they'll go, for a warming cup of tea
'It's getting on for four o'clock, it's nearly time to go'
The little bus is waiting, the driver at the door
A mother with her tired brood is hurrying down the road
She's had a busy shopping day and struggles with her load
It's been a lovely outing to the little market town
The farmer had a brand new saw, his wife will have a gown
They all are settled in their seats, they're off without a fuss
Away they go, it's homeward bound in the cosy little bus.

Barbara Davies

WINTER'S PICTURE

It seems to me that long ago,
We had in winter - lots of snow.
And when you see some pictures old
With piles of snow - don't they look cold?

These lovely pictures I can see
On the table in front of me.
Takes me back to when I was young,
And in the snow had lots of fun.

Tradesmen's carts went slithering by,
Ladies with their skirts held high.
Lots of space for children to play
That was before the motorists' day.

Dads' made sledges from bits of wood,
With children helping when they could.
Tiny tots could just about cope
Polishing the runners with soap.

To the park the youngsters would go,
To test their sledges on the snow.
Returning home all rosy red,
Just in time for supper and bed.

Smoke would curl from chimneys tall
Icicles hanging from the wall,
Roaring fires to keep us all warm,
Blow the snow, we'd weather the storm.

Old memories come so very clear,
About that lovely time of year,
I'm glad the painter's captured all,
The beauty of 'cold winters' fall.

Isobel Crumley

STREET URCHIN

I shivered, pulling my threadbare coat so tight
With dull, lacklustre eyes, gazed at the scene before me
People going home to their warm fires, they were all right
Didn't have to sleep in a doorway and starve like we.
We the forgotten ones, no one cares
They don't see us as they stare
But we are human the same as they
They may blink, but we won't go away
All that we dream of, fresh loaf of bread
Without it, we may end up dead.

Dora Watkins

A MOMENT CAST

Snow bells echo the winter sky,
people calling passing by, foot
prints mark a moment past, on
virgin snow a moment cast.

muffled hooves on cobbled street,
shadows walk on silent feet,
grey forms pass 'neath naked
limbs, eyes downcast, as twilight
dims.

'neath chariot wheels, lies
beauty scarred, what music to
the ancient bard, who sits alone
on rooftop high and sings to
shadows passing by.

but silver shines where shadows
tread, no darkness now, till
winter's dead.

Jim Cuthbert

One Christmas

Safe journey my love I wish you well
You won't return your eyes did tell
What did I wrong this Christmas tide
What made you go and not abide?

When you arrived I took your coat
Your voice seemed strange, so remote,
Is there another in your life
Who will take you for his wife?

Goodbye my darling, happy Christmas dear
The street's so much colder now you're not here
Hope you liked my gift, I shall treasure yours
I can't stop the tears, must hurry indoors.

Richard Youngs

A Rim Of Snow

Back to back, the figures move away,
In waisted coats, tall hats,
The past strolls down a snowy street -

A downcast lady, parting company with a gent
Who hides his hurt, his face a fixture,
Has turned her back on marriage and a home,
To write the stories singing in her head.

Once widowed, living in a single room,
She rocks her child in narrow circumstance.
Were she to wed, she knows her freedom
Would not last; her hand, be stilled.

Her new typewriter, prized possession,
Gives her power to rush her task.
Her skirts will shorten as the quick years pass,
While written pages flow in every season.

But now, a carriage rumbles by,
To disappear far in the distance,
Like the man she has rejected,
Like the comfort she dismissed.

A jaunty youth in cap and jacket
Thinks to throw a snowball at the horse,
From an avenue of barren trees -

A scene of uprights, with a rim of snow
On geometric buildings of the town,
Fixed forever, a black and white still,
Emotions hidden in the people caught in motion.

Marian Reid

The Spirit In The Street

The spirit in the street lifts couples hearts,
As they pass by slowly in a horse and cart.
Adjacent trees iced with the snow,
Stand tall and silent with a sparkling glow.
Trails of footsteps and wheels scurry fast,
Imprint a white quilt as they create a past,
Of early morning businesses, exchanges and trade,
Preparing for Christmas and presents to be made.
Strangers in the road, exchange glances as they pass,
Smile welcome thoughts before midnight mass.
Carols muffle from the end of the road,
To an audience hypnotised in a swaying mode.
Steam slowly rises from in-between the rooftops,
People wander around and in and out of shops.
An odd chorus of barking pollutes air from peace,
Then diminuendos to a final decease.
The sky is choked with winter's clouds,
No breath of blue is seeping around.
Children's laughter heard in a family home,
Stared at from outside by people unknown.
Half past the hour and all is still,
All life has left and the street is tranquil.
A slight chill whips throughout the trees,
A sign of the spirit, who is finally pleased.

Tor

THE ROYAL THEATRE: COPENHAGEN - DECEMBER 21ST 1879

The front door slammed
And shock waves surged and heaved and whirled:
The critics damned
As ink, like raging waters, swirled
In protest
And countless
People talked.

The front door slammed
And shudders shook society:
A woman's hand
Had, the laws of matrimony,
Contravened.
Women dreamed
When Nora walked.

Diane Elizabeth Maltby

Late Date

Standing with hands in pockets, the man impatiently waits,
A date he had arranged but already the lady's late.
Now he is cold, pacing the wintry street to and fro,
If it snows anymore he thought I will just have to go.

He takes out his fob watch, to look once again at the time,
But all he can picture is his lady's face in his mind.
Suddenly, slowly trudging along through snow on the ground,
Hears someone carefully trying not to make steps resound.

And there approaching our man, is the lady in question,
'Difficult to walk in snow,' she says, 'with high heeled boots.'
'Let us get out of here and find somewhere pleasant for tea,
Know I said we'd meet at quarter to, now it's half past three.'

S Mullinger

WINTER WEDDING

'Twas winter in Paris, a snow laden street
She hurries to cross it, her lover to meet
But the carriage sped past her,
The hoofed horse was fleet.

A bitter cold morning, skies hung low and grey
With no hint of sunshine on her wedding day
She glanced all around her, bleak buildings, bare trees.
Where had the spring gone with warm summer breeze?

Where was she going and how would she fare?
And what if no carriage arrived to get there?
Oh, what if her lover has tired of the wait
Along comes the carriage with horse slow of gait

She watches the creature come to his slow halt
Her heart beats like thunder, her nerves strained and taught.
Her gown and her bonnet are not at their best
One glove she has lost and her hair is a mess
But a fire in her heart burns with soft rosy glow
She alights from the carriage, steps down into snow.

'Tis winter in Paris and there stands her beau
The ice in her heart has melted in pride
Her lover is waiting to greet this his bride.

Hazel Brydon

Christmas Shopping

Louisa plods doggedly on through the snow,
Whatever the weather, she's determined to go
To complete her gift shopping list today:
She must get her parcels sent on their way.

The carriage ahead, would be warmer, of course,
Quite exciting too, with a smart, trotting horse,
But her Christmas cash has been thought out with care;
Sadly, there's no room for luxury there,
So, on to the shops, she's content to roam
And happily loaded, she'll wend her way home!

Vera Sykes

My Island Paradise

Transport me to an island,
Far away from daily life,
Surround me with a paradise,
Apart from all the strife.

Sapphire sea and emerald trees
Flowers of every hue,
A hut amongst the shimmering sands,
And, interruptions few,

Delight me with sweet music,
Drifting through the sky,
Caress me with glowing sun rays,
That radiate from high.

Give me peace of mind and soul,
Where I can dream all day,
Transfer me to '*Utopia*',
Take my cares away.

Lynda Fordham

Dancing With Love

(Inspired by Jack Vettriano's painting
'Dance me to the end of love')

Dancing with love in the moonlight,
On a wet and silver beach.
Knowing that your love for me
Is only just out of reach.

White crested waves, caress the shore,
The moon's reflection, shows me heaven's door.
I will dream that you hold me, as I walk on air,
And I don't need to see you, to know that you are there.

Imaginary arms around me, showing that you care,
The breeze blowing gently, kisses my face,
And adds a magical touch to this peaceful place,
In my imagination, I know you are there!

Gliding softly, dreaming with glistening eye,
Remembering the happy times of days gone by.
Misted forever now, with the passing of years,
When you were there, to wipe my tears.

The touch of you, like sand, through my toes,
The smell of you, like the perfume of a rose.
Lingers on, a never-ending story,
Keeping you in my heart, an ever present memory.

Anne Roberts

Memories

I get a funny feeling,
When the air is fresh and sweet;
When I walk across a meadow,
Feel the grass beneath my feet.
I get a funny feeling,
When I stare out in distance,
Down a disused railway track.
I get a funny feeling,
When I'm lying in my bed,
And the rain runs down the window,
Playing tunes inside my head.
I get a funny feeling,
Sitting on a train,
And the rattle of the engine,
Jogs memories in my brain.
Life is full of fading memories,
And glimpses of the past;
Doubts about the future,
Which hopefully won't last.

Suzie Vanderborght

PLACE OF DREAMS

My place of dreams,
A cocoon of quietness,
Enfolding and enclosing me,
Yet setting me free.
Allowing me to be what I want to be,
Exciting me, delighting me,
Inviting me into a bright new world
The magic world of imagination.
My *Special* place, my *Secret* place
Within *Me*.

Mary Hodges

On The Road To Garda

On the road to Garda
from Calais down through France
Across the Strasbourg border
thro' Switzerland we pass - and
All those mighty mountains - high
in the Italian Alpines with
Miles and miles of vineyards everywhere

Along the road to Riva - a -
round the shores we roam - with
Miles of market street stalls
selling many things - unknown
Windows full of flowers
everywhere we go - and
Everyone's on holiday - like you!

A magic trip to Venice
a city full of dreams - a
Coffee in St Mark's Square - a
must - to be seen! Be-
Neath the Bridge of Sighs - a
romantic trip in a gondola! - re-
Calls a song about a -
famous Cornetto!

Staying at Torbole - our
Hotel Holiday - and
Strolling by the Lakeside - in
the cool evening air
All those mighty mountains - re-
flected everywhere - a
Picture to remember - at
our holiday hotel!

Nelson

HEY JUDE

It's only a few years since 'Hey Jude' was our song,
time goes so fast, though it doesn't seem long.
You were my little one, still finding your way,
although even in those days, you still had a lot to say.
You were born in our home, with us all around,
I tried so hard to get the twins, not to make a sound.
I know thinking back, that those were happy days,
life was so good yet simple, in so many ways.
We had a house, a car and a good life to boot,
everything was so exciting, life was a hoot.
I don't really know, what happened from there,
at least you are still around, to love and care.
You will always be with me, deep in my heart,
although we often are, so very far apart.
So on this special day, my thoughts are with you,
I love you, happy birthday, 'Hey Jude'.

Ken Mills

THOUGHTS AND WISHING WELLS

Only thoughts and wishing wells
And little babies small
Fairy stories, nursery rhymes
My mother read them all
She told us tales of long ago
About her growing years
Such changes she had shared through life
Her many hopes and fears
She loved us
Taught us many things
Remembered through the years
We miss her love and tenderness
But still know that she's near
Now as the years have come and gone
Our thoughts are ever true
Of wishing wells and babies small
We've shared a lifetime through.

Jeanette Gaffney

WONDER OF SUNSET

Flashes of glory not her own
Adorned, apparelled in celestial light
A golden, rustic, mystic, magical sight
Dazzling, blinding momentary bright
A miragic splendour of sunset's might

Caressing, enticing my inner self alight
Soothing, healing my blighted heart
Balms for my weary, worn heart
A reverent, infectious wonder
Hallowing a fleeting interval
Of the day's luminous moments

Blending, magical prismatic rays
A lasting setting miracle
A blue tinge in the grass so green
Shades of green in a face so white
Blue - whiteness, a milky way
Of things quiet, clear, connected
In the wonder of sunset.

George Saurombe

By The Sea

Thousands of sparkling silver lights,
Flickering on the sea,
Transport me to the very heights
Of summer ecstasy.

Whispering waves caress the shore
As the strong sun blazes down.
Who could wish for anything more,
Far from the noisy town?

Grasshoppers chatter and butterflies fly
Over this peaceful scene.
Seagulls swoop and then glide by,
All is at peace, all is serene.

I sit on a hill above the beach,
Enraptured by all I see.
Dreaming of horizons, beyond my reach,
Dreaming of what I might, but never will be!

Sheila Dodwell

TABLE MOUNTAIN

Table Mountain, a natural wonder
A mountain of many temperaments
Sometimes stark and foreboding against an angry sky
Always unique when cloud formation floats across
The flat surface and spills over the sides like a tablecloth
Ready to display a feast for giants
Other times alluring, set against a blue sky and
Bright sunshine thus inviting mortals to explore its secrets

I succumbed to this invitation
Within a glass domed cable car, I soared to the summit
I was not disappointed

Breathtaking views over Cape Town and far beyond
Left me spellbound - an artist's dream
Flora and fauna proudly displayed their presence
Inquisitive dassies peered out from behind boulders
Tame enough to accept food from an outstretched hand
Lizards scurried over rocks and disappeared into crevices
Exotic flowers grew and blossomed in stony soil

I wandered along a rugged path until I found myself alone
I sat upon a rock to breathe in the fresh cool air
Silence engulfed me, except for the murmur made by
The bustle of the world below
I was content and time stood still

Eventually I came aware of my solitude
With regret I retraced my steps to rejoin the human race

I will return to Table Mountain one day
To me it is Utopia, my place of dreams.

Sheila Wyatt

DREAM TOWERS

Towers dominate
The travel weary mind
From super-gothic
Massive spire
To squat cupola
Blown by Norfolk winds
Bizarre towers
Of myriad shapes and forms
Are scattered through
A dark mysterious park
And in the haunted woods
Of childhood years
A ghostly folly
Hides a cloudy moon.
Asian temples built to heathen gods
Stand overgrown in rainy Midland skies
The stately Parthenion old as time itself
Awaits a squad of crack athenian troops

Paul Wilkins

DOLPHIN FANTASY

I walk along the lonely beach; it shimmers in summer's heat
With every step its golden sand ripples beneath my feet
A lazy, calm and lapping tide plants kisses on the shore
While above my head the white, wild seagulls gently rise and soar
I stand to drift in dream; feel my eyelids fall and close
Then lay my sleepy body in the peace of soft repose
Now floating in the ether, I leave reality behind
  to take my favourite seat within the cinema of my mind
Upon the screen the sea is set with diamonds on its face
Lit by summer's sunlight; a twinkling tidal race
Quite suddenly they scatter as if were pushed aside
  to make a path for silver darts rolling on the tide
Leaping, twisting, turning, here dolphins are at play
  and moving ever closer on this glorious, magical day
I hear across the water sweet voices calling me
As brother and sister dolphin sing their song of Mother Sea
My head now fills with coloured sound which only I can hear
Compelling me to follow them; to trust and not to fear
'I cannot gentle dolphin, for I am of the land'
'O simple human trust us now, come we shall guide your hand'
I hesitate; then follow; for compulsion says I must
  when instinct drums incessantly, the dolphin's message 'trust'
Then soon I'm gliding through the waves just as the dolphin swims
My lumbering human form is cast, my legs, my arms are fins
And as I laugh and play with them in games of Dolphintime
  I feel their healing pulse of love deep within my mind
But all too soon the moment comes when both of us must part
For I must now return to land where lies my human heart
They guide me to the shallows where once more I shall don
  the trappings of that human form my life depends upon
Restored to human likeness now I watch across the bay
With the magic of my inner eye I can see them glide away

A summer wind collects my thoughts to carry on the air
  a message to the dolphins for each of them to hear
'I will not say goodbye my friends, for in my reverie
  I know I can relive . . . my Dolphin Fantasy.

Joan Robson

THE OLD MILL

The mill seemed magic in my young years
Saying 'Come and see me, please' -
A place which we would see from home
Peeping through the trees.

Across the loch we rowed to it
Father, mother, me -
Bringing all our picnic food
Of sandwiches and tea.

The July day was sultry
When we tied up on the shore;
The air was filled with scents of trees
And insects by the score.

We filed through head-high bracken
And came upon a lawn
Behind which stood the ruin itself
Suggesting times long gone.

So still and peaceful was this place
To ponder on the past,
With overhanging trees all round
And burn gurgling fast.

Nearby there was a lochan
Where water-lilies curled,
The silence there was so profound -
Secluded from the world.

The overlooking oak-clad hill
Made the glassy water black -
A home for coots and herons,
To this spot I now think back.

Marjory Scott

God's Garden Of Love

G lowing gardenia, colours' bright
A marylis, anemone, ash and aconite
R oses, red bud rhododendron
D ahlia, daffodil, daisy, delphinium
E delweiss, elm, evening primrose
N ature's way to say how I love you so

My ideal world is in God's garden of love
Relaxing in the land of dreams.

Laird P Brewer

PERHAPS

One day, perhaps,
I'll travel far;
Pillow my head
On a falling star:

Follow the trails
Of the milky way,
Where bright moonlight
And planets play:

'Mid sun and moon
Bathe in the glow,
Searching for dreams
That I have known:

I'll skim the clouds
And touch the sky,
While eons of time
Go drifting by:

See my maker,
Tell my story,
And wonder at
The distant glory:

'Tis there I will,
With heaven above,
Live out my dreams
And wait for my love.

H Val Horsfall

LET THERE BE LIGHT

O God, when you said let there be light,
You did not mean wars to rage and fight.
It must make you feel so very sad,
When you see your world has turned so bad.
The world's become very dark and grim,
With people who do not recognise Him.
He came to give good news to the poor,
Who chose His kindly words to ignore.
But there are those of us who do hear,
The words of our Lord whom we hold dear.
Father may He soon return again,
To free this world from anguish and pain.
I do not think you will stand much more,
Watching those who rage then make war.
I believe soon you'll come to release,
Those who love you and desire only peace.
Father in Heaven please hear my prayer,
There is so much darkness everywhere.
Come back Lord in your infinite might,
And restore to your world, your glorious light.

Nicky Young

PEACE

Oh, restful sea, on peaceful day,
Where golden sunbeams dance, and play
With lapping wavelets, on the strand
Of pebbles, shells and golden sand.

Where many a shady, cool, retreat -
With mossy couch and grassy seat,
On sultry day - refreshing - cool
That overhangs some 'phantom' pool.

There oft in childhood days to peer,
From rocky ledge, through water clear;
With 'dreamy' thoughts of fancy's flight
To caverns deep, with mystic light.

Orion sends his violet ray,
There ghostly fishes, glide and play -
Amongst the seaweed - dart and gleam,
In fairy caves of emerald green.

And fairies, pixies, little elves,
Tell 'special' tales - on rocky shelves -
In whispers low, of wealth untold
Of amber, coral, pearls and gold.

Until awakened from my dream
By plaintive 'hoot' of ship's siren,
That calls the pilot from afar,
For escort o'er the harbour's bar.

Then - fishing boats, that dip, and glide
Come sailing home, on flowing tide,
To rest at anchor, by the quay -
With silver harvest from the sea.

Now; soothing tones of gentle wind,
Convey a peace to heart and kind,
And as of old they sing to me -
The glories of a summer sea.

Marjorie Lancaster

Dreams

There is a place I dream of, it's a place of dreams indeed.
For it's a place where there's no enmity or greed.
It's a place where everybody is contented with their life
And you don't see any cruelty, no trouble and no strife.
Of course it's just a dream but wouldn't it be great
If the world was full of love instead of jealousy and hate.

T Ingram

A Place Of Peace

A place of peace and nature's own tranquillity
where whispering of breezes sway tall trees and birds
call out in song and lapping ripples round the lily pond
all blend in sunlit harmony of sound -

Where migrant slickers from dark city blocks drop in
To ease their loads, slow down the pace and smooth away
their stress, like long haul flocks to dip in dapple light
and bask upon the sleepy slopes of timelessness -

To seek some calm and coolness for fraught minds
and wander aimlessly the woodlands wild, as when a child
to drink the sparkle stream of hope and in the soothing
stillness of this scented place to find themselves -

And then to come across a painted chapel hidden in
the trees, a secret presence vibrant in their midst
where they might 'hear' how He had seen their needs
and brought them to this haven to receive His peace.

Rosemary Keith

SCENE FROM LUSS PIER

Ben Lomond in the distance
On a clear sunny day
Water on the Loch
Smooth, peaceful you could say
The picturesque scenes
Attract the crowds
To the end of Luss Pier
To capture the beauty
Of mountains, greenery and Loch
On Camera to keep
A wonderful memory of Scotland
That will never sleep

P Edwards

My Place

My dreams would thrive near meadow side
of boys and girls in love
of parties and of discos
and of Heaven above.

Such harmony in school friends' kisses
in warm days and in all well wishes
a place where we saw Paradise
surpassing richest words of vice.

Christine Jacobs

Grandma's Cottage

Searching for paradise
- I found it for sure
In quiet serenity
At Grandma's back door

Folk dashing off in cars
All chasing the crowds
But Grandma and I
Just sat watching the clouds

Beneath pink perfumed roses
- 'Twas any artist's dream
Here Granny would serve us
Jam scones and cream

Wee robin came hopping
For crumbs at our feet
He knew Grandma's cooking
Was always a treat!

Birds of all species
Serenaded the dawn
And what fun they had bathing
In the bath on the lawn

How sweet Grandma's cottage
Hers - a heavenly life
Just a mother - grandmother
And an old fashioned wife!

Norah Page

My Dream

I long for my homeland
A seat by the hearth
The glow of the fire
The old dog on the mat,
Food on the table
Warm clothes on my back,
This is my dream
As I lie in the park.
Why did I wander
On that sunny day?
The grass seemed greener
As I stole away.
My bed a park bench
Cardboard rough on my back
An old sack my blanket
As I long for the dark.
Lord, don't let it rain
I can't bear the pain
Of joints that creak
I am tired and weary
And longing for sleep.

Marie Kelly

THE KENTISH DOWNS

When you leave the dusty highways and byways
And enter again the fresh country pathways,
The wind and the birds in the trees bid you welcome.
Spotlights from heaven make to forest look golden.
Through the fields of bluebells, hops and wildflowers
To the old pill boxes now covered in brambles.
Next the babbling brooks, lakes and cascading streams
Where a dragonfly plays with the fish and the bees.
Country walks, parks and old village houses
Time stands still and tradition is thriving.
From a crumbling wall to the sky through the trees
See Doe church, the druid stones and our history.
The Pilgrims walk through the Kentish Towns
Are just some of the things that make the Kent Downs.

Ann-Marie Williamson

The Carousel

Roll up, roll up,
Come ride the carousel,
It's a journey of dreams,
Climb up and I'll tell.
Choose your white steed,
Adorned in beads and gold,
Hold tight to the reins,
Let the magic unfold.
Untie your ribbons,
That tether your hair,
Toss back your head,
Let the enchantment start there.
Close your eyes tightly,
Now the ride will begin,
Let the horses ride faster,
Feel the soaring within.
Let your laughter echo,
Don't keep it inside,
Let your hair fly wildly,
Now open your eyes.
Do you see them?
The stars, green, blue and red,
Circling above you,
Dancing all around your head.

Claire Partridge

MY DREAMS

I once had a dream to reach a star.
That I could fly ever so far.
To have such a dream to come true,
I don't know what I would do.
To wake up in the morning
I find what is left.
The shine of a pound at the end of my bed.

Rebecca Padbury (9)

HOW CALM IS THE NIGHT

How wearying was the day,
But how calm is the night:
The conflicts of the daylight
Have extinguished each other,
And now tenderly follows the peaceful night.
Some souls are already in dreamland,
Whilst others are hovering.
Clouds scarcely delineated
Seem to be the comforting
Of a heavenly blanket:
A moonbeam now slants through,
So lightly kissing the church spire,
Before losing itself in the mellowness of the night.
Silently, dark shadows, stand and lean about,
Giving unwavering assurance in their cloaking:
All feels well -
How calm is the night.

John M Reeve

Ballerina Gardenia

When garden flowers sway in dance
their gender is always feminine;
so strong in bright freshness
on stems they support with love
to display beauty with elegance.

There, perfume lingers in moist air
among the harlequin roses
against the azure backdrop of sky.

Here, with floral agility she enters
nimbly with brilliance of balance,
lithe, lissom, lyrical.
As a breeze wafts the grass heads
her movements swing diaphanous strands.

Her finely expressive limbs wed
athletic passion to music's precision.
Her steps blend in artistic fusion.

Stunning as vernal blossom
vibrant as a Chopin chord
irresistible as curling surf
memorable as lovers' kiss
light as an airborne feather

the ballerina, poised, enpetalled
drops within her folded arms
to be curtained still as a grounded leaf.

Dennis Marshall

FOOLPROOF

My castle should I build it
would have walls a mile wide,
secret tunnels without number
where ghosts and goblins hide.
A thousand turrets would stab the sky
each one ludicrously tall,
every one a book within itself
for me to read them all.
From the centre would rise a solid mass,
a great black brooding keep,
along its roof the living proof
that here the dragons sleep.
Inner sanctums would blaze with light
on all the hundred floors,
strange music echoing off the stones
as above my spirit soars.
No place of gloom would be my room
bright blue on every wall,
a fortress impregnable even to time
for what is never built cannot fall.

M Morris

My Bird Has Flown

All grown up now
Independent
Up and left the rest
My baby bird has flown.

Travelling
Unravelling
The wonders of the world
My baby bird has flown

She comes back for a short time
But off she goes again
Hopping on and off the plane
My baby bird has flown.

It's not a life that I have known
My baby bird has flown.

Theresa Hartley

DREAMS

A panoply of thoughts,
a cacophony of sound and light
playing on the mind's eye -
like a juicy fruit about to burst.

The remembrance flown away
as morning breaks in pieces;
before the mind can grasp it
and follow it to understanding.

Where did it go? beyond infinity?
will it return sometime? or not at all.
the same? or will the next be changed
so I will not know the meaning.

Will it be fulsome, brave and whole
to glorify the wandering soul?
not warlike, dark and despairing;
let me wake with a smile.

Patricia Davies

Ode To S'Illot

(A village in Mallorca)

I dream of summer evenings, watching sunsets in S'Illot,
My tiny heaven here on Earth, a little place that time forgot.
The peaceful setting summer sun seems to sink into the bay,
Waves lapping gently on the beach, at the end of another day.

I sit upon the rock by the tiny harbour light.
Watch fishing boats returning home, unload, then tie up for the night.
A gentle breeze gives freshness to the Mediterranean eve.
As the moon ascends in heaven high, I slowly take my leave.

With the dawning of another day, I take a languid walk,
See a friend upon the sandy street, and of course, we stop to talk.
Shutters slowly open from overhanging balconies above,
In this place of tranquil memory, touched by the hand of Him above.

In timeless contemplation, I would watch the palm trees sway,
Smell the orange blossom in the air, watch dragonflies at play.
Fragrant bougainvillea provide a drink for lazy bees,
And all the world is far away, across the seven seas.

'Buenos dias mi amigo', comes the cry from many quarters,
I'm accepted here, no more a stranger, in this place by tranquil waters.
A lotus eater's paradise, how I wish that I could stay,
Here among my many friends, for ever and a day.

I would feast upon the freshest fruits, and the harvest from the sea,
Sip your wine, enjoy siesta, in peaceful tranquillity.
Here, the air is clean and fresh, life lived at a gentler pace,
I'd face each brand new morning with contentment on my face.

But this is just my dream alas, my hope for what may be,
If only one fine day would dawn, when I could live here by the sea.
To feel the warmth of the sun upon my back, to sit and watch
the world go by,
To close my eyes, hear the waves on the shore, and bid my cares
goodbye.

Brian L Porter

Dreaming

My dream is floating on a silver cloud
With golden edges all around
Through the rush of time.
Higher, higher up we climb
Bright and shining stars go by.
Keeping up their pace we try
Awaking now, my mind a blur,
I wonder did this dream occur?

A Dutschak

One Of My Dreams - Jamaica

Sun sea and sand,
Jamaica is the place I can't wait to land,
an eight hour flight,
land in Jamaica, where it's nice and bright,

People walking bare feet down the street,
in their cloths and rags,
carrying their scandals bags,
off to the down town market,

Market men and women brawling,
saltfish, bread fruit, ackee,
open unuh bags,
gi mi a $100 dolla

Then in the night,
it is bashment time,
when people go out to wine and dine,
dress to kill,
even those who haven't paid their bills.

Shantel Faure (17)

MAKE PLANS

I'll call you in the morning,
And call you at night,
Blow my kisses out of the window,
Talking until my echoes reach you.
I'll run to find you -
I'll be your queen
And my fingers touch the water,
I'll see your reflection in the stream,
When at last you're there,
I'll know that you care
Like a single snowdrop
You'll be precious.
A star is a wish,
That may come true.
A jewel studded element,
In a night so blue.
You'll be my king,
In the day, in the night,
I won't give up my loving
It's not just a dream.

Sarita Wooten

A Magical Kingdom

In a time long ago,
In a land far away.
Wonders of the past,
We do not see today.

Wizards painting rainbows,
While fairies play beneath.
White knights riding horses,
With roses in their teeth.

Mermaids sit upon the rocks,
Lure sailors to their doom.
Goblins and witches,
Dance around the room.

Where unicorns and dragons,
Roam across the land.
In a kingdom full of magic,
Together we will stand.

J M Judd

A New Day Will Dawn

The world has turned a murky grey
no hint of sun like yesterday.
No song of birds to charm the air,
just gloom and darkness everywhere.

The vase of flowers upon the table
looks tired and faded, as if unable
to fill the room with fragrance sweet,
missing now the sun to greet.

But gloom will pass, and come again
the sunshine's warmth, and gentle rain,
new growth will spring amidst the showers
that bring new life to summer flowers.

On treetops high the birds will sing,
or on the summer breeze take wing,
and where the world was dull and grey,
sweet warmth will charm the gloom away.

M Ward Hunt

The Glow-Worm

On balmy summer nights in the cool grass
Deep in dark thickets where air softly swings
Perfume from every flower,
Where whirring wings
Of moths brush dusty pollen as they pass,
Within this dell I light my little lamp
Of golden-green, and all around me there
A hazy glow hangs green-gold in the air.
Magic the midnight hour.

Midsummer night: the short warm darkness
When my light
Shines steadily amid the silver-white
Of dew-drops on the grass blades and pale flowers
Silver as stars:
All still,
Although so fast the passing of the hours.

For wanderers here,
Seekers of beauty by the sea or streams
Or mountains their high summits ringed with stars,
The singers and the dreamers, some of dreams
Unfading, unlike rainbows, or the dew
Invisible in air,
I light my lamp
And shine as I have shone since long ago,
My steady green-gold glow,
My tiny light,
Part of the timeless wonder of the night.

Diana Momber

Scottish Highlands

Travelling to the Scottish Highlands,
With rolling hills, and piping bands,
The River Dee, goes on for miles,
With waterfalls, and deep rock piles.

Such peace and beauty everywhere,
We can only stand and stare,
The sheep and deer, just roaming free,
Red squirrels, chasing up a tree.

We come upon small Craithie Church,
And enter there, to say a prayer,
The organ playing a favourite hymn,
You can feel the peace within.

Then we cross the River Dee,
Balmoral Castle for to see,
In wandering round those Castle grounds,
Imagination, knows no bounds.

At night, a highland laddie singing,
The pride within his voice is ringing,
Of his clans, and bravery rare,
In battles fought, and lassies fair.

We say goodbye, to this fair land,
Of mountains, lochs and castles grand,
Getting home in time for tea,
Back once more to reality.

Ivy Griffiths

Sky Over Durham

Oh how beautiful the sky was this night,
Did you see the sun like an orange ball so bright?
The cast of its magical glow so soft and serene,
Taking life from reality into a dream.
Then all too quickly darkness draws near,
And the sun wet over Durham slowly disappears.

Pam Cook

DAYDREAMS

There's a dream I've had for quite a while
To take a trip down the 'Nile'
While sweeping leaves up with my broom
I dream of 'Tutankhamun's tomb
And while I'm doing the washing up
I think about the land of 'Tut'
The 'Pyramids' I'd love to see
Instead of pictures on TV
To look upon the face of 'Sphinx'
And stand and wonder what he thinks
The 'Valley of Kings' I'd love to stroll
Or where they found 'The Dead Sea Scrolls'
To ride a camel across the sands
Of this wonderful and ancient land.

While round the supermarket I roam
I'm dreaming about 'Cleopatra's home
And pushing the trolley out to the car
I'm wandering in some Eastern Bazaar
With bright coloured carpets and smells of spice
Unusual fruits and all kind of rice
How I would love to see first hand
The glory of the 'Pharoes' land
To sail the waters of the Nile
With the ever watching crocodile
Some day my daydreams may come true
And I will visit these places new
Until then I'll keep on trying my luck
With hope one day my numbers come up!

Valerie Hillier

DREAM MACHINE

And when I dream -
I only dream of
Mundane things,
Exasperating nights
Of skeletons past
Clinking around in
A semi-dormant mind.
It's as if a policeman
From my subconscious
Has caught up with me;
Confiscated my
Dream machine and
Put it under lock and key.

Alan Holdsworth

Reverie

They promised I wouldn't have nightmares,
so you must be encroaching my dream.
You've got to leave now, I'm caught unawares.
Stop haunting, you're not what you seem.

They said I'd forget and your fancies would go.
And my mind wouldn't play games again.
So you must be a dream and I want you to know,
that I'm not playing host to insane.

Sara Ann Alcraft

THE MAGIC SYMPHONY

The mist rolls in, gently caressing the sand,
As a wave runs ashore and plants a kiss on the land.
The sea bird screams as it dives and swoops,
Through rushes so moist, they bend and they droop.

The dawn of a day, the darkness retreating,
A glimpse of a pale sun, albeit but fleeting.
The breeze is soft, the sky mostly grey,
Crabs scurry sideways, and the dolphins play.

The sounds of the sea, like a magic symphony,
Thunders and crashes, drums and tympani.
Rocks standing proud, try to hold back the tide,
Like giants they stand, with arms open wide.

So it has been, since time began,
A tribute to nature, no help from man.
With majestic beauty, she reigns supreme,
This is her world, Nature is queen.

Keith Johns

From A Very Foreign Field

These are the memories I cherish.

A day still with blue, heavy with roses
peaceful and green.
Sunbeams surfing the corn
moving like waves on a deep blue sea.
Willows doodling idle shadows on the river
all homespun coats and colours.
A generous warmth caressing the air,
a courting thrush testing his sound on the morning
and me, a child of long ago
taken by the hand
fingers tuned to a Braille of memories
as I ramble again the country lanes of England.
And I smile at this wonderful peaceful land
as memory thrusts greatness upon it.

L Williamson

Jewel Of The Green Heart

High in the rolling Umbrian hills,
A panoramic picture spread below,
Lies a town unspoiled,
Of compelling character,
Rich in countless treasures.

A community at peace,
Still and tranquil
In the fresh mountain air.
A consecrated place.
A pilgrims' Mecca.

Here at the shrine of St Francis
Travellers kneel
And marvel at the genius of Master Artists,
Whose priceless colours, though sullied,
Surround him in his glory.

Assisi should be the last place to visit.
By comparison others pale.
Here I felt welcome.
Here I felt good.
Here I felt God.

Stanley Longbottom

IDEAS FOR DREAMS

Dreams for Einstein
Came in numbers.

Dreams for Schweitzer
Came on a jungle beat.

Dreams for Visionaries
Came in the light of stars.

Dreams for young lovers
Came on a blackbird's song.

Dreams for children
Rushed in on the wings of horses.

Dreams at the death bed
Tiptoed in on a soft dove's wing.

Gabrielle Hopkins

THE SECRET PLACE

In my dreams I go to a secret place,
A secret place with a familiar face,
For it always seems that the place of my dream
Is one that I know from long ago
In my waking hours I once was there
Just once, but when was this? And where?
From my memory's edge recollection takes flight.
And I cannot recapture it, try as I might
I hope I go there again tonight.

It is not a garden, my secret place -
But it is a garden green
Sweet and green serene,
Serene and still - tranquil
Tranquil and calm, a pastoral balm,
That eases the stain of the real world space
Contented I lie where safe ground gently slopes,
And dream in my dream of desires and hope
Here trouble recede, all burdens grow slight,
And yesterdays where some problems seem trite
I hope to go there again tonight
I pass through a hedge, the hedge has no gate.
For who would create - even contemplate
A secret place with a beckoning gate?
There's no 'entry' sign to this place of mine
No 'This way please', no duplicate keys
Here I'm alone, but never lonely,
For I know that I am only
A thought away from the moment, I'm gladly bereft
And I must leave my place when the time is right
But I hope I gather in my dreams again tonight.

M S Cornbill

Perfect Peace

The gentle scent of meadow grass
and sunshine in a cloudless sky,
a distant lake that shines like glass,
fond memories as years go by.

Eyes shut, just listening to each sound,
each moment precious, gone so fast,
knowing there's beauty all around,
if times like this could only last.

Birds and bees, fragile butterflies,
fly and flit, their colours aglow,
shimmering as the heat starts to rise,
relaxed, at peace, no wish to go.

A tractor in the field beyond,
scattering grass ready for hay,
a lonely duck pecks at a frond,
playful squirrels head for their drey.

Myriad insects hurrying by,
carrying burdens twice their size,
wondering where they go and why
they manage with such enterprise.

Daylight fading, the sun sinks down,
shadows lengthen, dimming the light,
colours so vivid, now seem brown,
perfect day gone, welcome the night.

A Odger

A Place Of Perfection

A place of perfection would be for me
Everyone living in true harmony
No fighting, no hunger, no poverty to see
All living a life, as it really should be

Caring and sharing, taking the time
Showing concern for both heart and mind
Loving each person whoever they may be
The colour the creed, one just wouldn't see

Instead one big family all living in love
Living each day the way we all should
Pulling together making things work
No dark corners of mind where evil thoughts lurk

Causing envy and rebellion, spitefulness and greed
Trying to outdo each other . . . instead of seeing 'the need'
To work together as God's family
This would be sheer perfection for me

Jean Beardsmore

These I Love

The marsh in all her moods is like a magnet.
She draws me back and makes my soul delight.
The oyster-catcher's cry is mystic music;
The sky a hemisphere of changing light.

The woods are never-failing founts of solace;
Each leaf a marvel and each branch sublime.
The air beneath the trees is nature's incense
And every track a path outside of time.

The mountain-top is far above man's influence
With eagle's view of river, lake and wood.
The rocky shore accepts the huge sea's pounding,
Exhilarating all who feel its mood.

So who could choose a favourite from such riches,
Or claim that any one is less than fine?
In every one there's life - enhancing spirit;
In all we have a glimpse of the Divine.

Carol Burton

IN MY DREAMS

I flew across peaks as an eagle,
soaring and circling on high.
To fly as a bird I would always try
- but I gave up my wings just for you.

I've played as a famous musician
on all the world's theatres and stage,
I lived for the cheers and devotion
- but the praise that I crave is from you.

I've discovered the rivers and oceans,
and swam with the sharks and seals,
I've talked to the whales and the dolphins
- but I came back to listen to you.

I've trekked across deserts and forests
on horseback or camel or mule,
I've lived amongst Indian tribesmen
- but I'd rather lie down next to you.

I've been the head of a nation
a hero so proud and so true,
on balcony I wave to my people
- but for an encore I'd sooner have you.

As a handsome desirable playboy
amongst models and actresses too,
I've courted the rich and good looking
- but I'd rather wake up next to you.

In my dreams I was looking for affection
for beauty and honesty too,
for action romance and a partner
- but in reality - there was always just you.

Harry Lees

Our Special Place

Places are like people,
full of heart
and full of soul;
so when you've found
your special place,
you cannot let it go . . .
It weaves its magic
all around you,
it's in every step
you take,
It leaves it mark
on you forever,
the cycles hard
to break.
And do you really
want to?
when you love this
place so much,
It's all you've ever
dreamed of,
it has the Midas touch . . .
We all have such a place,
if only in our hearts,
and I can never leave it,
I guess I knew that from
the start . . .

Jade Watkins

Valley In Mist

Wet grey cloud rolls down the mountain
swallowing as a cetacean quaffing krill
the slag of the abandoned lead mine
turning slate grey the deepening gloom.

Tendrils spread across the valley floor
derelict buildings lost in the mist
rivulets of water flow down the tent
a candle flame drips light around the flap.

From inside the tent, sitting quietly,
spectres dance amongst the billows
shape and form obey only chaos
a living, moving kaleidoscope in panorama.

Quiet, solitary listening
a twilight zone, within but not part of
the world moves on, circling the sun
the valley remains timeless, without change.

Robin Colville

Clovelly Walk

A niche in a hillside - still'
and nowhere found but on a slope a smooth
pebbled lane descendingly stepped, winds
down to a quay: to a seagull's shrill.

Stilted white cottages to a rock face cling;
huddled yet quaint they peel time away and the pall
of honeyed scent waits for a breeze,
if this place were dreams they'd be dreams for a king.

A worn metal lock guards a fisherman's home;
how many before me pushed its dark
heavy door, no one to greet but dusty sunlight
dipped to a corner soulless as stone.

Stillness it seemed could not release the past;
its story laid on cold dull walls witness to
a stoic life,
where joy and tears ran so fast.

Aloof as a squire but would he stay;
brushed my hand a grey twirling cat - he moves
as if lost will he follow me,
but smoke stack wisps gave folk away.

Cane lobster pots and nets far behind;
under the bridgehouse more breath to my stride to a
staunch chequered quay like a fortress immersed,
as ancient a paradise as I would find.

On a tree capped shore I sat and thought back;
men of toil who'd faced their storm, their women
waited as providence provides: surely I thought
what could these stalwarts lack?

Proud folk on a hillside still - today;
beyond them changes
but not their kingdom forever proclaiming,
my presence fulfilled: away, away.

Tom Griffiths

THE DREAM

I had the strangest dream the other night,
I saw an angel shining bright,
An open book held in his hands,
In which he wrote in golden bands.

I studied him with great delight,
As curiously I watched him write,
And as he made a further note,
I asked him what it was he wrote.

He looked at me as there I lay,
And then it was I heard him say,
'I write of those who can afford
To say with pride, I love the Lord'

I lay there in my earthly bed,
And thought awhile before I said,
'Put me down with your golden pen
As one who loves his fellow men.'

He wrote - and in a flash was gone,
But returned before the night was done,
I guess I must have passed the test,
Because my name led all the rest.

G K (Bill) Baker

THRONE OF THE GODS - OLYMPIA

Ancient temple, ruined shrine,
Say what mystery divine
Still rules here in majesty?
In this wreck of time immense
What assurance of the sense
Whispers immortality?
Still the former splendours show,
Still the oak and laurel grow
By the King of Heaven's throne;
Near the leafy groves arise,
Shaded from the cloudless skies
Which Apollo calls his own.
Through the columns seems to ring
In the pine trees echoing
Song of the competing lyre;
The course still rumbles with swift feet,
Forms where strength and beauty meet,
Burning with a manly fire.

Hear, you Powers Olympian!
For a day prolong your span,
Bring again the ancient glory,
Write a new and nobler story.
Hearts in love with beauty yearn,
To your temple, Zeus, return!
Let your nectar touch our tongue,
Make us all forever young.

Barrie Williams

Ode To My Beloved America

Troubadours, poets, writers and dramatists
I wish to intone with you an ode to my America
Venerated ancestral land, three seas honour your beauty
Motherland in you I trill, cradle of my ancestry and birth

Oh American continent . . . Paradise of warrior races
Sioux, Apaches, Aztecs . . . Mayans, Incas and unconquered Araucanians
Brotherhood of ancient cultures, light, science to the modern world

Land of high peaks, deserts and jungles, tapestry of pined valleys
Flamboyantly coloured wildlife, luscious palm trees and sun

Entangled forest, nest of anacondas, papagayos, toucans, piranhas
Mighty flows run through your body, crystal nectar blood of life
Delightful, voluptuous America, so much of your radiance in my mind

Oh usurped beloved continent, receptacle of conquistadors and evil-doers
Turquoise Caribbean waters, swashbuckling seas of buccaneers
Tomb of sunken Spanish galleons and their stolen treasure

One with the Pacific blue, serene ocean of your history
Garden of food for the Gods and sons of struggles and glories

Kissed on the East by the Atlantic, christening your rising sun
Ocean of orphaned emigrants, seeking for a new motherland
Continent of exuberant geography, jealousy keeping in your core
Streaks of most precious metals, copper, silver, emeralds, gold . . .

Oh beloved America of my birth, indomitable poetic song
Daring exciting adventure, amongst natives of your womb
Exotic, fertile abode of flamingos, llamas, pumas and condors

With my ode I travel deep, to a sacred land on the south
Kingdom of Caupolicán, Galvarino, warriors of bronze and stone
'Arauco', pride of my heart and soul . . . Never conquered by the Conquistador

Still lost in the thoughts of my journey, I come to the land of the cold
Scattered white crystal glaciers, fairy tale of a world beyond
Home of penguins and walrus, end of my travel and prose
Oceans embraced in an oath, sentinels of your secrets and love

Eduardo Del-Rio Escalona

Silence Of The Paths

Mount Snowdon is quiet right up to the peak,
there's been no one up there for many a week,
all paths are closed down from north, east and south,
because of the plague that's called foot and mouth.

The paths are all silent, grass grows from the sod,
the tracks once quite busy, now no one has trod,
a place once alive with school children's loud chatter
is silent and empty, no boots pitter patter.

Walking the highway is just not the same
dodging the traffic is not a safe game,
it's out in the country on that I'll agree
looking down from the summit, is the best place to be.

Up there in the mist, in the wind and the rain
chatting to tourist who came up by train,
then walking the ridge, just a few inches wide
not able to hurry nor take a long stride.

Sometimes it is wet and sometimes it's sunny
but no matter the weather I still think it's funny,
at times there's mist and my feet barely see
other times snow, that's well over my knee.

But the views from up there is one to behold
it's worth all the effort and even the cold,
the silence is broken by birds, wind or plane
and once paths are open, I'll go up again.

Leslie Holgate

A TRIP TO INDIA

I feel the heat the most at midday,
Ice cold drink from a straw please.

People continue in their daily business,
Some are on bikes others hard at work.

'What colour madam?' The shopkeeper asks,
I am baffled as there are so many to choose from.

The city of colour I call it,
Although I haven't seen Holi.

A loud voice of a boy catches my attention,
The boy is pushing a stall with Dosa and other cooking equipment
on it.

I focus on the young boy's face.
I can smell the aroma of the Dosa.

I pardon myself and leave the shop.
I head towards the Dosa stall. To my surprise the boy greets me
with a smile.

I request for a Masala Dosa,
To which boy responds quickly.
To my surprise there are a variety of types of Dosa,
The young boy is an expert,
Back at home we would call him a chef.

The Dosa is piping hot chilli too,
I take a bite and my taste buds go wild,
The amount of flavours I can taste in an instant is incredible.

Suddenly a man pushes me who is on his bike,
I turn to pull a face to show my annoyance.

I return to the Dosa boy but he has vanished.
The thought crosses my mind that
I forget to pay!

Parveen Kaur Saini

Eternity

The shadows lengthen and the sun sinks low,
And in the evening light the roses glow,
And climbing up the trellis arch they make
A tremulous reflection in the lake.

And underneath the arch there is a seat,
A peaceful and an undisturbed retreat,
Where I on summer evenings take my book
Away from the harsh world to this lone nook.

But on this balmy eve, as I come near
My resting place, I see a figure here
Clothed all in white and dazzling to my sight,
So that I drop my book in sudden fright.

The figure rises and I hear his voice:
'You need not fear, but rather should rejoice.
I am your guardian angel and I come
To take you to your everlasting home.'

'Then I must die,' I answer in dismay,
'And never see another summer day.'
He takes my hand: 'Not die, but live in bliss,
Where this world's beauty you will never miss.'

I look into his eyes, and written there
I see the truth about that land so fair,
Where Christ is king and blessed spirits dwell,
And peace will all anxiety dispel.

And so I hold his hand and with him rise
Into the clear and sunset-tinted skies,
And all eternity is mine to share
Unending joys and love beyond compare.

Constance Driver

A Place Of Dreams

(A Green by the sea at Yarmouth, Isle of Wight)

Peace, tranquillity, sun dappled sea
Time to reflect with a picnic tea.
The cry of a seagull, waves gently lapping,
In a parked car - an old couple napping.
The breeze gently blowing the leaves
The mist in the distance covers the trees.
A man with a shrimp net leisurely paddling
The roar of a powerboat westwardly travelling.
Wightlink ferries crossing the Solent
A billowing spinnaker, somebody rowing.
An elderly lady walking her dog
A lively young couple enjoying a snog.
A girl on a bike riding the footpath
Children playing, having a laugh.
A young family out for a stroll -
I sit on a bench quietly watching them all.
A bank of cloud temporarily screens the sun
Folk going home now - the day nearly done.
Most people have gone home, into town,
But I'm going to sit here and watch the sun going down.

Jackie Holland

OUR FISH POND

Placed with care in partial shade,
Rocky backdrop set with plants,
A little water-world we've made,
Where lilies spread, as sunlight slants.

Fountain plays with restful sound,
Rippling, tinkling, splashing spray;
Here, sweet solitude is found
From restless world on arduous day.

Blades of iris guard a clutch
Of jellied tadpoles, seething dots;
Nodding heads, narcissus Dutch
Cluster round in random lots.

Goldfish glide like submarines,
Surfacing for floating flakes;
Contrast sharp with equine greens
As each one its morsel takes.

O'er the surface, insects shoot -
Water boatmen, hov'ring flies -
But hidden depths keep frog and newt
Quite safe from piercing, preying eyes.

In this secret world below,
Photosynthesis decants
Pure oxygen, dispersing slow,
Freed by vibrant, waving plants.

Shall we tarry yet awhile,
Lost in pleasant mem'ries fond?
We'll have reason oft' to smile,
Resting by our own fish pond.

Gareth Wynne Richards

To Be At One

(This poem is dedicated to Joy and Kenny.
This was written on day four of my first visit to Sanday.
It was written on Backaskail Bay.)

I sit on a deserted shoreline
Alone with my thoughts,
Seeing for the first time the
Beauty that surrounds me.
Distant cries from the birds pierce
My thoughts, as I tingle with warmth
As I am caressed by nature.
The winds encase me stripping
Away negative thoughts that have
Harboured here for too long. Hurt
And pain sink into the sand beneath me.
I lap up the energy and charge
My soul; my spirit revived
I walk again with nature.

Chrissi

Enjoy The Beauty Of The World

Enjoy the beauty of this world, it's there for all to see,
The sun, the moon, the tiny stars, the mountains and the seas.
The trees, the flowers, the singing birds, and all the meadows green,
The deserts with their golden sands, rivers, and the rippling streams.
Animals and the reptiles roam, in forests, swamps, on mountains steep,
Fish swim in our garden ponds, in rivers, lakes and oceans deep.
The mountains challenge you to climb, and lift you from your gloom,
The songs of birds to give you cheer, hark to the melody and tune.
Be thankful for your presence here, amidst the world's majestic scene,
Your mind will photograph the views, for the album of your dreams.
Enjoy creative works of man, silhouetted in the skies,
Cathedrals, castles, towering tall, elegant beauty for the eyes.
Parks and cottage gardens with roses climbing walls,
The buzzing of the honey bees, collecting pollen on their calls.
Let flowers bring a smile to cheeks, enjoy their perfumed scents,
The pages of your album turned, peaceful moments now well spent.
When life's pressures take their toll, and you begin to feel the strain,
You may long for some escape, that may relieve you from the pain.
Glance in the album of your mind, a short while every day,
It will give you peace and strength, to journey on life's way.
Enjoy the beauty of this world, it's there for all to see,
To each and every one of us, nature gave it to us free.

Donald Futer

A SECRET, QUIET, PRIVATE PLACE

It was a secret, quiet, private place.
A little dell of green and mossy grass,
And a small pond where ponies came to drink.
The trees and bushes hid it from public view.
Few but some locals knew that it was there,
Yes, it was such a quiet, private place!
We lived on Dartmoor then, most days we'd walk
Together along the path from our house gate.
How well I know each feature that we passed!
We loved to stop there at the little dell.
It was our secret, quiet, private place.
Alas, it is more private to me now . . .
They gave me a jar of ashes, and I thought;
'Where else should they be scattered but the dell,
Within our secret, quiet, private place?'
I went there again today as usual
To somehow prove love's annual pilgrimage.
Of course, as last year, you weren't there again,
And never again can be. Yet I stood
Revolving all our memories in my mind,
With a few renegade, insistent tears.
And then I left our quiet, private place
And went back to the silent, empty house
Purged, to begin another empty year . . .

J D Goodspeed

DREAMING

Wind in spray
mist like a cloak
grey wings of gulls
storm slumbers

dark an age ago
around rocks a shawl
green seaweed, motion
long shadow swimming

moon/sun in my soul
coldness stone strokes me
flames in morning
sun rising high above

snowy flutter of spray
swans soar and sing
gulls sail on lonely errands
sunrise rekindles gold on rocks

world sheathed in frost
cold ocean caressing me
nets sing with blue fish
that rise through rainbows

lightly as pebble skims pond
gulls cry lonely distress
I am launched into airy spray
I become a ghostly shell

rocking in early waves

T Webster

My Special Place

In my garden is a special place
It's a corner where I sit and daydream -
Of the day when I wore white lace
On our wedding day.

The years have gone by -
Our children have grown,
Our daughters have sons of their own,
I, think of them all with a sigh!

As I sit there in the corner, all alone
My mind wanders to days long ago -
Memories, good and bad, happy and sad,
And our precious son, who's a really fine lad.

The special place in my garden
Is where my partner is laid to rest.
We lost him just after Christmas
It was such a terrible shock.

C Cook

A Dream Of Boats And Lakes

(Holiday on the Norfolk Broads)

Alone at last
How the time goes fast,
So quiet and serene
How I long to dream

To drift in a haze
On these lazy days,
Relax as we must
Everything like problems,
Turn to dust

To sail away, on a sunset lake,
And feel the heat, from the sun's rays
So calm the waves, on these lazy days

But dreams never last
As the time goes so fast,
To come back to reality,
And hit normality

Until next year
The dream of boats and lakes,
Seem so far away
But once again,
Are adrift in a haze
On these lazy days

Sharon Christian

SEA-LOCH

Night's soft shadows fade away
Into thin mists of silver-grey.
Pale gold skies of sunlight come
With the rising of the sun.
Mist on the water rolls away
Before the warmth of early day.
On smooth waters, summer light
Dazzles, dances, yellow bright.
Across the loch a playful breeze
Moves the water, blows the trees.
Slap, splash, the waters go
Against the rocks that line the shore.
Ripples along the tiny beach
Make little birds fly out of reach.
An early sea-bird skims along
Flying low, no call, no song.
Splashing tide, the birds, the trees,
The only sounds on the summer breeze;
And salty fresh there comes to me
The tangy scent of open sea.

Haidee Williams

A Special Place (Park - Co Wicklow)

The view from every window flaunts green acres - sky - the sea
Soft pastel stranded white puffed clouds above each weathered tree
And silence - save the murmur of the breeze; one chirping bird
Sings welcome through the springtime air, though nothing,
not one word

Escapes the lips of those who've come so far to try regain
Tranquillity - an inner peace, alleviate the strain
Of city life - the business place which cannot quite compete
With nature's wiles sojourning in this heavenly retreat.

Tomorrow we will walk the beach, meet no one but the tide
And seaweed-covered grey stone rocks as eagerly our stride
Will cross the space where tiny shells and pebbles straddle sand
Confronting where both surf and foam come rushing in to land

And bare white feet will be awash - the salt spray through our hair
As body soul and mind relax by simply being there
Amidst the power of nature's force - we'll want for nothing more
Than what exists along that stretch of enigmatic shore

And always this immense allure will beckon from afar
Come visit me, I'll help re-find the person that you are
Escape awhile the stressful life - yes you can find a way
To opt out here, what's mine is yours for ever and a day

Jo Lewis

Days Gone By

Sometimes when we are young
We sit and maybe dream
Of things that have now passed
Of things that could have been

But who knows in the years ahead
May some of them come true
And bring a special meaning
To me and maybe you

For dreams are truly wonderful
Of days or even years
Some of them of laughter
Some of them of tears
As through the years we go along
And older then we get
Have we forgotten dreams gone by
No, not even yet

So spare a while to sit and dream
Of days that now have gone
Dreams of joys that there have been
As through life we travel on

L E Davies

SECRET PLACE

The warm brush of summer breeze
The tunnel of green pine trees
The pine needles under feet
The secret place, where we would meet
I loved him - I think he knew
The breathless climb, the scenic view
Glints of sun - light up his face
Is heaven on earth, such a place?
Not a moment's time to waste
His body bare, his warmth, his taste
Soon this hour, will be gone
Lost in the blackbird's song
How quickly, time will pass
Flattening the velvet grass
Mother Nature, or Mother Earth
What, I wonder, is she worth?
She blends into the scenery
It is only her I see
Our time has only just begun
Soon the two, will be one.

Carol Mogford

NIGHT JOURNEY

Late night transport
from the city
steady traffic
        open roads

ever changing
neon colours
kaleidoscopic
        suburbs pass

blinding headlights
blink and dazzle -
hail or thunder
        rain or shine

lines of red lights -
cars, vans, lorries -
lead us onward
        up the hill

where: a beautiful vista with orangy balls
never-endingly shrinking to dots of bright light
        - in the dark -

isolating us here, so it seems time stands still
implanting the scene way down deep in my mind
        - or it's lost -

towns and country
then our village
lighted windows
        just whizzed past

dreamy passenger
we've arrived now
with reluctance
        I get out.

Dorothy